DWIGHT L. MOODY

The Best from All His Works

OTHER AUTHORS IN THE SERIES

DWIGHT L. MOODY

The Best from All His Works

Dwight L. Moody
Abridged and edited by Stephen Rost

THE
CHRISTIAN
CLASSICS
COLLECTION

Publishers since 1798

THOMAS NELSON PUBLISHERS
Nashville

Contents

DWIGHT L. MOODY

Introduction

Dwight L. Moody (1837–99) is, along with Billy Graham, one of America's most celebrated evangelists. He was part of a rapidly growing heritage of preaching in America: the traveling evangelist. After the Wesleys, Whitfield, and Finney paved the way in earlier days, Moody came on the scene to continue the evangelist movement with outstanding success.

Moody did not have the type of childhood one would consider conducive to raising successful children. His father was an alcoholic and eventually died from his addiction. He left the large Moody family heavily in debt. Eventually creditors took most of what they had, leaving the family destitute. The kind help of a Unitarian minister enabled the family to begin recovering, but they were never far removed from poverty.

Moody did not receive a thorough education because of family problems. His religious training was even worse. Around the age of seventeen, Moody left his home in Northfield, Massachusetts, and went to Boston, hoping to find a job in his uncle's shoe store. At first the uncle was opposed to such an arrangement, but he later agreed on the condition that Moody would live where he was told, abstain from drinking and other vices, and attend church. This arrangement forced Moody to attend the Mount Vernon Congregational Church, and he was converted in 1855.

Seeking greener pastures, Moody arrived in Chicago in 1856 and became a shoe clerk. Later he worked as a salesman and debt collector. These jobs enabled him to save thousands of dollars. But his heart was in the ministry, and in 1859 he organized a Sunday school mission which became quite successful. This led him to give up secular work and become a full-time minister. He became involved with the YMCA and was a popular speaker at city-wide revival meetings and other engagements.

With his popularity soaring, Moody engaged in traveling evangelistic work. This took him to the eastern United States as well as England.

But his influence did not stop with the pulpit. His deep concern for education led him to establish several schools for girls and boys. And his greatest legacy was the Moody Bible Institute, founded in 1886 in Chicago.

Moody died in 1899, leaving behind a rich life filled with great success, not only as a winner of souls but also as an educator of minds.

Faithfulness is an important characteristic in any Christian. The Bible is full of examples of individuals who were used by God because they were found faithful. In this message Moody stresses the importance of being a faithful worker in God's vineyard.

He begins by telling about his long years in the ministry and the fact that God has been a faithful employer. The pay of the ministry is far greater than silver or gold, and the sooner one gets involved, Moody says, the better. Throughout the sermon he supports his claim with examples of people who have had fruitful ministries.

Moody believed effective ministry could be developed in groups of any size. Often he encountered people who taught small groups of boys and girls. Such people felt that their work was not important, but Moody always assured them that even the smallest numbers were valuable. In his mind, the tiniest group could contain a potential Luther or Wesley. He emphasized this over and over again to any teacher who came to him with a defeated countenance. To Moody, obedience, not size, was the standard set by God and the measure of a Christian's faith.

CHAPTER ONE

The Reward of the Faithful

I want to call your attention to the fourth chapter, gospel of Saint John and part of the thirty-sixth verse: "And he that reapeth receiveth wages and gathereth fruit unto life eternal." I want you to get the text into your hearts. We have a thousand texts to every sermon, but they slip over the hearts of men and women. If I can get this text into your hearts today, with the Spirit of God, these meetings will be the brightest and most glorious ever held in Chicago; for it is the Word of the Lord, and His Word is worth more than ten thousand sermons. "He that reapeth receiveth wages." I can speak from experience. I have been in the Lord's service for twenty-one years, and I want to testify that He is a good paymaster—that He pays promptly. Oh, I think I see faces before me light up at these words. You have been out in the harvest fields of the Lord, and you know this to be true. To go out and labor for Him is a thing to be proud of—to guide a poor, weary soul to the way of life, and turn his face towards the golden gates of Zion. The

Lord's wages are better than silver and gold, because He says that the loyal soul shall receive a crown of glory. If the mayor of Chicago gave a proclamation stating that he had work for the men, women, and children of the city, and he would give them a dollar a day, people would say this was very good of the mayor. This money, however, would fade away in a short time. But here is a proclamation coming directly from the throne of grace to every man, woman, and child in the wide world to gather into God's vineyard, where they will find treasures that will never fade, and these treasures will be crowns of everlasting life; and the laborer will find treasures laid up in his Father's house, and when, after serving faithfully here, he will be greeted by friends assembled there. Work for tens of thousands of men, women, and children! Think of it and the reward. These little children, my friends, are apt to be overlooked; but they must be led to Christ. Children have done a great deal in the vineyard. They have led parents to Jesus. It was a little girl that led Naaman to Christ. Christ can find useful work for these little ones. He can see little things, and we ought to pay great attention to them.

As I was coming along the street today I thought that if I could only impress upon you all that we have come here as to a vineyard, to reap and to gather, we shall have a glorious harvest, and we want every class to assist us. The first class we want is the ministers.

There was one thing that pleased me this morning, and that was the eight thousand people who came to this building, and the large number of ministers who seized me by the hand, with the tears trickling down their cheeks, and who gave me a "God bless you!" It gave me a light heart. There are some ministers who get behind the posts, as if they were ashamed of being seen in our company and of our meetings. They come to criticize the sermon and pick it to pieces. No effort is required to do this. We don't want the ministers to criticize but to help us and tell us when we are wrong. There was one minister in this city who did me a great deal of good when I first started out. When I commenced to teach the Word of God I made very many blunders. I have learned that in acquiring anything a man must make many blunders. If a man is going to learn any kind of trade—carpenter's, plumber's, painter's—he will make any amount of mistakes. Well, this minister, an old man, used to take me aside and tell me my errors. So we want the ministers to come to us and tell us of our blunders, and if we get them to do this and join hands with us, a spiritual fountain will break over every church in the city.

Many ministers have said to me, "What do you want us to do?" The Lord must teach us what our work shall be. Let every child of God come up to these meetings, and say, "Teach me, O God, what I can do to help these men and women who are inquiring the way to be saved," and at the close of the meetings draw near to them and point out the way. If men and women are to be converted in great meetings, it is by personal dealings with them. What we want is personal contact with them. If a number of people were sick, and a doctor prescribed one kind of medicine for them all, you would think this was wrong. This audience is spiritually diseased, and what we want is that Christian workers will go to them and find out their trouble. Five minutes' private consultation will teach them. What we want is to get [to] the people. Everyone has his own particular burden; every family has a different story to tell. Take the gospel of the Lord to them and show its application; tell them what to do with it, so as to answer their own cases. Let the minister come into the inquiry room.

An old man—a minister in Glasgow, Scotland—was one of the most active in our meetings. When he would be preaching elsewhere he would drive up in a cab with his Bible in his hand. It made no difference what part of Glasgow he was preaching in; he managed to attend nearly every one of our services. The old man would come in, tenderly speak to those assembled, and let one soul after another see the light. His congregation was comparatively small when we got there, but, by his painstaking efforts to minister to those in search of the Word, when we left Glasgow his church could not hold the people who sought admission. I do not know of any man who helped us like Dr. Andrew Bonair. He was always ready to give the weak counsel and point out the way to the soul seeking Christ. If we have not ministers enough, let those we have come forward, and their elders and deacons will follow them.

The next class we want to help us to reach the people is Sunday school teachers, and I value their experience next to that of the ministers. In the cities where we have been, teachers have come to me and said, "Mr. Moody, pray for my Sunday school scholars," and I have taken them aside and pointed out their duties and shown how they themselves ought to be able to pray for their pupils. Next meeting very often they would come, and the prayer would go up from them, "God bless my scholars."

In one city we went to, a Sunday school superintendent came to his minister and said, "I am not fit to gather sinners to life eternal; I cannot be superintendent any longer." The minister asked, "What is the reason?" and the man said, "I am not right with God." Then the minister advised him that the best thing, instead of resigning, was to get right with God. So he prayed with that teacher that the truth would shine upon him; and God lit up his soul with the Word. Before I left that town, the minister told me all doubt had fled from that superintendent's mind, and he had gone earnestly to work and gathered, from the time of his conversion, over six hundred scholars into the school of his church.

The Lord can bless, of course, in spite of schools and teachers; but they are the channels of salvation. Bring your classes together, and pray to God to convert them. We have from three thousand to five thousand teachers here. Suppose they said, "I will try to bring my children to Christ," what a reformation we should have! Don't say that that boy is too small or that girl is too puny or insignificant. Everyone is valuable to the Lord. A teacher, whom I found at our services when she ought to have been attending to her class, upon my asking why she was at our meeting, said, "Well, I have a very small class—only five little boys." "What?" said I, "You have come here and neglected these little ones? Why, in that little towhead may be the seeds of a reformation. There may be a Luther, a Wheaton, a Wesley, or a Bunyan among them. You may be neglecting a chance for them, the effects of which will follow them through life." If you do not look to those things, teachers, someone will step into your vineyard and gather the riches you would have.

Look what a teacher did in southern Illinois. She had taught a little girl to love the Savior, and the teacher said to her, "Can't you get your father to come to the Sunday school?" This father was a swearing, drinking man, and the love of God was not in his heart. But under the tuition of that teacher, the little girl went to her father and told him of Jesus' love and led him to that Sunday school. What was the result? I heard, before leaving for Europe, that he had been instrumental in founding over seven hundred and eighty Sabbath schools in southern Illinois. And what a privilege a teacher has—a privilege of leading souls to Christ. Let every Sabbath school teacher say, "By the help of God I will try to lead my scholars to Christ."

It seems to me that we have more help in our revivals from young men, except from mothers, than from any other class. The young men are pushing, energetic workers. Old men are good for counsel, and they should help, by their good words, the young men in making Christianity aggressive. These billiard halls have been open long enough. There is many a gem in those places, that only needs the way pointed out to fill their souls with love of Him. Let the young men go plead with them, bring them to the tabernacle, and don't let them go out without presenting the claims of Christ. Show them His never-dying love. Take them by the hand and say, "I want you to become a Christian." What we want is a hand-to-hand conflict with the billiard saloons and drinking halls. Do not fear, but enter them and ask the young men to come. I know that some of you say, in a scornful way, "We will never be allowed to enter; the people who go there will cast us out." This is a mistake. I know that I have gone to them and remonstrated and have never been unkindly treated. And some of the best workers have been men who have been proprietors of these places and men who have been constant frequenters. There are young men there breaking their mothers' hearts and losing themselves for all eternity. The Spirit of the Lord Jesus Christ asks you to seek them out. If we cannot get them to come here, let the building be thrown aside, and let us go down and hunt them up and tell them of Christ and heaven. If we cannot get a multitude to preach to, let us preach, even if it be to one person. Christ preached one of His most wonderful sermons to that woman at the well; and shall we not be willing to go to one, as He did, and tell that one of salvation? And let us preach to men, even if they are under the influence of liquor.

I may relate a little experience. In Philadelphia, at one of our meetings, a drunken man rose up. Till that time I had no faith that a drunken man could be converted. When anyone approached he was generally taken out. This man got up and shouted, "I want to be prayed for!" The friends who were with him tried to draw him away, but he shouted only louder, and three times he repeated his request. His call was attended to, and he was converted. God has power to convert a man even if he is drunk.

I have still another lesson. I met a man in New York, who was an earnest worker, and I asked him to tell me his experiences. He said he had been a drunkard for over twenty years. His parents had forsaken him, and his wife had cast him off and married someone else. He went into a lawyer's office in Poughkeepsie, mad with drink. This lawyer proved a good Samaritan. He reasoned with him and told him he could be saved. The man scouted the idea. He said, "I must be pretty low when my father and mother, my wife and kindred, cast me off, and there is no hope for me here or hereafter." But this good Samaritan showed him how it was possible to secure salvation, got him on his feet, got him on his beast, like the good Samaritan of old, and guided his face toward Zion. And this man said to me, "I have not drunk a glass of liquor since." He is now leader of a young men's meeting in New York. I asked him to come up last Saturday night to Northfield, my native town, where there are a good many drunkards, thinking he might encourage them to seek salvation. He came and brought a young man with him. They held a meeting, and it seemed as if the power of God rested upon that meeting when these two men went on telling what God had done for them—how He had destroyed the works of the devil in their hearts, and brought peace and unalloyed happiness to their souls. These grog shops here are the works of the devil—they are ruining men's souls every hour. Let us fight against them, and let our prayers go up in our battle, "Lord, manifest Thy power in Chicago this coming month." It may seem a very difficult thing for us, but it is a very easy thing for God to convert rumsellers.

A young man in New York got up and thrilled the meeting with his experience. "I want to tell you," he said, "that nine months ago a Christian came to my house and said he wanted me to become a Christian. He talked to me kindly and encouragingly, pointing out the error of my ways, and I became converted. I had been a hard drinker, but since that time I have not touched a drop of liquor. If any one had asked who the most hopeless man in that town was, they would have pointed to me." Today this young man is the superintendent of a Sabbath school.

Eleven years ago, when I went to Boston, I had a cousin who wanted a little of my experience. I gave him all the help I could, and he became a Christian. He did not know how near death was to him. He wrote to his brother and said, "I am very anxious to get your soul to Jesus." The letter somehow went to another city and lay from the 28th of February to the 28th of March—just one month. [When he received it,] he saw it was in his brother's handwriting and tore it open and read the above words. It struck a chord in his heart, and was the means of converting him. And this was the Christian who led this drunken young man to Christ.

This young man had a neighbor who had drunk for forty years, and he went to that neighbor and told him what God had done for him, and the result was another conversion.

I tell you these things to encourage you to believe that the drunkards and saloon keepers can be saved. There is work for you to do, and by-and-by the harvest shall be gathered, and what a scene will be on the shore when we hear the Master on the throne shout, "Well done! Well done!"

Let me say a word to you, mothers. We depend a good deal upon you. It seems to me that there is not a father and mother in all Chicago who should not be in sympathy with this work. You have daughters and sons, and if work is done now, they will be able to steer clear of many temptations and will be able to lead better lives here. It seems to me selfishness if they sit down inactive and say, "There is no use in this. We are safe ourselves, what is the use of troubling?" If the mothers and fathers of the whole community would unite their prayers and send up appeals to God to manifest His power, in answer to them there would be mighty work.

I remember in Philadelphia we wanted to see certain results, and we called a meeting of mothers. There were from five to eight thousand mothers present, and each of them had a particular burden upon her heart. There was a mother who had a wayward daughter, another a reckless son, another a bad husband. We spoke to them confidently, and we bared our hearts to one another. They prayed for aid from the Lord and that grace might be shown to these sons and daughters and husbands, and the result was that our inquiry rooms were soon filled with anxious and earnest inquirers.

Let me tell you about a mother in Philadelphia. She had two wayward sons. They were wild, dissipated youths. They were to meet on a certain night and join in dissipation. The rendezvous was at the corner of Market and Thirteenth streets, where our meetings were held. One of the young men entered the large meeting, and when it was over went to the young men's meeting near at hand, and was quickened, and there he prayed that the Lord might save him. His mother had gone to the meeting that night, and, arriving too late, found the door closed. When that young man went home he found his mother praying for him, and the two mingled their prayers together. While they were praying together the other brother came from the other meeting, and brought tidings of being converted, and at the next meeting the three got up and told their experience. I never heard an audience so thrilled before or since.

A wayward boy in London, whose mother was very anxious for his salvation, said to her, "I am not going to be bothered with your prayers any longer. I will go to America and be rid of them." "But, my boy," she said, "God is on the sea, and in America, and He hears my prayers for you." Well, he came to this country, and as they sailed into the port of New York, some of the sailors told him that Moody and Sankey were holding meetings in the Hippodrome. The moment he landed he started for our place of meeting, and there he found Christ. He became a most earnest worker, and he wrote to his mother and told her that her prayers had been answered; that he had been saved, and that he had found his mother's God. Mothers and fathers, lift up your hearts in prayer, that there may be hundreds of thousands saved in this city.

When I was in London, there was one lady dressed in black up in the gallery. All the rest were ministers. I wondered who that lady could be. At the close of the meeting I stepped up to her, and she asked me if I did not remember her. I did not, but she told me who she was, and her story came to my mind.

When we were preaching in Dundee, Scotland, a mother came up with her two sons, sixteen and seventeen years old. She said to me, "Will you talk to my boys?" I asked her if she would talk to the inquirers, and told her there were more inquirers than workers. She said she was not a good enough Christian—was not prepared enough. I told her I could not talk to her then. Next night she came to me and asked me again, and the following night she repeated her request. Five hundred miles she journeyed to get God's blessing for her boys. Would to God we had more mothers like her. She came to London, and the first night I was there, I saw her in the Agricultural Hall. She was accompanied by only one of her boys—the other had died. Toward the close of the meeting I received this letter from her:

Dear Mr. Moody: For months I have never considered the day's work ended unless you and your work had been specially prayed for. Now it appears before us more and more. What in our little measure we have found has no doubt been the happy experience of many others in London. My husband and I have sought as our greatest privilege to take unconverted friends one by one to the Agricultural Hall, and I thank God that, with a single exception, those brought under the preaching from your lips have accepted Christ as their Savior, and are rejoicing in His love.

That lady was a lady of wealth and position. She lived a little way out of London; but she gave up her beautiful home and took lodgings near the Agricultural Hall, so as to be useful in the inquiry room. When we went down to the Opera House she was there; when we went down to the east end there she was again, and when I left London she had the names of 150 who had accepted Christ from her. Some said that our work in London was a failure. Ask her if the work was a failure, and she will tell you. If we had a thousand such mothers in Chicago we would lift it.

Go and bring your friends to the meetings here. Think of the privilege, my friends, of saving a soul. If we are going to work for good we must be up and about it. Men say, "I have not the time." Take it. Ten minutes every day for Christ will give you good wages. There is many a man who is working for you. Take them by the hand. Some of you with silver locks, I think I hear you saying, "I wish I was young, how I would rush into the battle." Well, if you cannot be a fighter, you can pray and lead on the others. There are two kinds of old people in the world. One grows chilled and sour, and there are others who light up every meeting with their genial presence, and cheer on the workers. Draw near, old age, and cheer on the others, and take them by the hand and encourage them.

There was a building on fire. The flames leaped around the staircase, and from a third-story window a little child was seen who cried for help. The only way to reach it was by a ladder. One was obtained and a fireman ascended, but when he had almost reached the child, the flames broke from the window and leaped around him. He faltered and seemed afraid to go further. Suddenly someone in the crowd shouted, "Give him a cheer," and cheer after cheer went up. The fireman was [charged] with new energy, and rescued the child. Just so with our young men. Whenever you see them wavering, cheer them on. If you cannot work yourself, give them cheers to [spur] them on in their glorious work. May the blessing of God fall upon us this afternoon, and let every man and woman be up and doing.

Charity, or love, is the heart of Christianity. It was the very thing that brought Christ to earth to save human souls. For his text Moody selected the great love chapter, 1 Corinthians 13. In it the ingredient for true success rings loud and clear: a Christian must have true love for people if he is to successfully win them to Christ. No other motive will produce the same results or incur God's blessing.

Often Christians confuse duty for love. It is possible to function for a time out of duty, but only love will enable one to work with the fullest satisfaction and contentment. To be a Christian entails loving others and being willing to help all those in need. A loving spirit brings unity, happiness, and success. God is pleased with and able to work through the lives of Christians who love others.

CHAPTER TWO

Charity

You will find the text in the first verse of the chapter I read this evening—1 Corinthians, thirteenth chapter: "Though I speak with the tongues of men and of angels, and have not charity, I am become as sounding brass, or a tinkling cymbal." You, I have no doubt, wondered how it is that you have not met with more success. I think if I have asked myself this question once, I have a thousand times, "Why is it that I have not had greater success?" But I never read this chapter without finding it out. It is a chapter that every Christian ought to read at least once a week, I think with a great deal of profit. A man may be a preacher and have all the eloquence of a Demosthenes—he may be the greatest pulpit orator that ever lived, but if love is not the motivating power, "it is as sounding brass or a tinkling cymbal." A good many churches have eloquent ministers. The people go there and listen critically and closely, but there are no converts. They have wondered why. The cause has been the lack of love. If a minister has not got love deep in his heart you may as well put a boy in the pulpit and make him beat a big drum. His talking is like the "sounding of brass."

Failures to make converts in those churches are common, and the reason so many preachers have failed is because love has not been the motivating power. The prophet may understand prophecy and interpret it in such a clear way as to astonish you. I have met men and sat down beside them, and they would dig out the most wonderful truths out of prophecy which I could not see. I have sat at their feet and wondered at their power in this respect, and wondered also why it was that they were not blessed with more converts. I have sought the cause, and invariably found it was want of love.

A man, though he is deep in learning and in theology, if he has no love in his heart he will do no good. A man may understand all the mysteries of life, may be wonderful in seeking out truths, yet [he] may not be blessed by winning men. Paul says that though a man understand all mysteries, if he have no love his understanding goes for nothing; and he goes a step further and says that a man may give large sums to feed the poor, but if love does not accompany the gift it goes for naught in the sight of God. The only fruit on the tree of life worth having is love. Love must be the motive power. A man may give his thousands to the poor and get the gift written about in the paper, where you will see that he is a good philanthropic man, yet if love does not prompt the deed, it goes for nothing in God's sight. Many a man here is very liberal to the poor. If you ask him for a donation to a charitable purpose, he draws his purse and puts down one thousand dollars; if you come to him for a subscription for this or that theological seminary he will draw his check instantly; but God looks down into that man's heart, and if he has no love it goes for nothing. Some men would give everything they have—would give their body for what they think is a good cause—for some truth they've got hold of; yet there is no love in the act.

The main teaching of this chapter is that love must be the motivating power in all our actions. If our actions are merely performed out of a sense of duty, God will not accept us. I've heard this word "duty" in connection with Christian work till I am tired of it. I have come down to a meeting and someone has got up and asked a brother to get up and speak. After considerable persuasion he has got upon his feet and said, "Well, I did not intend to speak when I came down tonight, but I suppose it is my duty to say something." And it is the same with the Sunday school; many teachers take up classes from a sense of duty. There is no love in them, and their services go for nothing. Let us strike for a higher plane—let us throw a little love into our actions, and then our services will be accepted by God if love will be the motivating power.

I have an old mother way down in the Connecticut mountains, and I have been in the habit of going to see her every year for twenty years. Suppose I go there and say, "Mother, you were very kind to me when I was young—you were very good to me; when father died you worked hard for us all to keep us together, and so I have come to see you because it is my duty." I went then only because it was my duty. Then she should say to me, "Well, my son, if you only come to see me because it is your duty, you need not come again." And that is the way with a great many of the servants of God. They work for Him because it is their duty—not for love. Let us abolish this word duty, and feel that it is only a privilege to work for God, and let us try to remember that what is done merely from a sense of duty is not acceptable to God.

One night when I had been speaking in this way in London, a minister said to me after services, "Now, Moody, you are all wrong. If you take this word duty out from its connection with our works, you will soon have all the churches and Sunday schools empty." "Well," said I, "I will try and convince you that I am all right.

You are married?" "Yes." "Well, suppose this was your wife's birthday, and you bought a present of a book for her, and you went home and said, 'Now, my wife, this is your birthday, I have felt it my duty to buy something for you—here's a book; take it.' Would your wife not be justified in refusing it?" "Well," said he, "I think you are correct; she would be right in refusing it." That wife would want a present given her through love, not duty. What Christ wants is that we will work for Him because we love Him. The first impulse of a young convert is to love, and if a young man attempts to talk to people without [having] been won to Christ by love—without [having] been converted by the true spirit of the Holy Ghost—his efforts fall short of their mark. If he has been touched to the heart with the love of Jesus, the first thing he does is to shout out that love which is waiting for all hearts. Paul, in the fifth chapter of Galatians, tells you that the fruit of the Spirit is "love, joy, peace, long-suffering." That is the fruit of the Spirit. He commences this line with love at the head of the list, and if love is not the motive we have not been born of the Spirit.

Let us ask ourselves the question, "Is love the motivating power that urges us to go out and work for God?" This is the first question that we ought to ask ourselves. Without it a great deal of work will go for naught. The work will be swept away like chaff without it. Christ looks down and examines our hearts and actions, and although our deeds may be great in the eyes of the world, they may not be in His eyes.

Look at that woman in Jerusalem. All the rich people were casting in their treasures to the Lord. I can see the women and men come into the temple, some giving one hundred dollars, others giving three hundred dollars, and others putting in five hundred dollars, and if there had been newspapers in Jerusalem in those days, there would have been notices of these contributions. It would have [looked] very well in print. But by-and-by a poor widow woman comes along and puts in a humble two mites. I can see the Lord sitting at the treasury when that woman comes with her little all, and hear Him saying, "That woman hath given more than all of them." Why? Not owing to the large amount. No; but simply because it was love that prompted that woman.

The one great thing that the church lacks at the present day, and if you ask me to put it into as small space as possible I can put it into a word of four letters— and that is, "love." Show me a church in which the members love one another, and I will show you a church that is on fire in the cause of Christ. In it there is a revival every day for the twelve months of the year—the 365 days of the year are filled with continual manifestations of Christ's love. That is the lack today. There is luke-warmness—coldness one toward another. In Second Timothy Paul tells what Christians' lives should be— sound in faith, sound in love, and sound in patience. If a man is not sound in faith, we would draw his head right off; if he is not sound in faith, put him out. But let him be ever so unsound in love, he will be kept in. How many men are here in Chicago who are in churches and who are continually picking to pieces and slandering their brothers. They are continually going about finding fault with someone. They have no love.

Those who do not love in the way stated in this chapter, ponder well its meaning. Let the question go home to every heart here tonight: "Is there anyone I do not love?" If you are treasuring up in your heart any feeling of hatred toward any man or woman, God will not love you. You must be ready to forgive and love. I do not know that we could put up anything better on the platform than that motto that "God is love," and may it be burned into your heart. You say you love those who love you. Any black-hearted hypocrite can love those who love him. But what Christ wants to teach us is to love those that hate us and slight us. If you can only convince men that you love them, you can influence them. That is what we want to do in order to touch the hearts of those we come in contact with [during] the coming month. If one of us went to a bad man and said to him, "You are the worst man in Chicago," that would not touch him; it would only harden his heart the more. We want to go to him lovingly, and show him the love that Christ offers him. When the Son of man came into the world it was love that moved Him, and we will never do any good with anybody till our own hearts are touched with that same love. If we are not loving toward others they will not like us, and instead of trying to talk for Christ we had better keep away. A worker must win the hearts and affections of the people before he can do any effective work.

When in London, Dr. Arnott came down from Edinburgh to one of our meetings, and he told those people something—I don't think the Londoners understood him, but if they knew of farm life as I did, they would have known what he meant. He said, "When I was on my father's farm, when they wanted to teach a calf to drink, they would bring it to the pail and a man would dip his finger into the milk and put it into the calf's mouth, drawing his hand slowly away, and before you knew it the calf was drinking for itself. And so," he said, "if you want to win people to Christ you have to go lovingly to them and lead them gradually to Him." If you do not make people love you, you need not talk to them. Oh, that God may show you this truth tonight, that the great lever of the Christian is love! If a Sabbath school teacher does not love his scholars—if he goes to them as if it was a lesson he wished to get over, it will not be long before they find it out. They will see it in his eyes, in his face, in his actions.

And so, let us see tonight the necessity of having the love of God in our hearts, and so when we approach that drunkard or that gambler we can win him to Christ; and so that when you show him the gospel and tell him you want him to be saved, he will receive you with a welcome. If you go to him from a sense of duty you will make no progress with him, but if you go to him and talk of the love of Christ, and show kindness in your actions, he will hear you.

A minister in London said to me one night, "Mr. Moody, I want you to pray for a lot of people who will be at the meeting tonight"; and when I went there I saw in one corner a father, mother, and four or five children. And I prayed for them. When I got home I asked the minister about the family, and he said they had been won to Jesus by a smile. He said he was passing by a house in that city one day at the window of which a little child was standing. He liked children, and smiled to [the child] and bowed. This minister was in the habit of passing the house every day, and the second time he noticed the child again, and he smiled again. The next time there were several children there, and he smiled and bowed again. When he came again he saw the same children standing there, but he saw a lady standing with them. He thought it would not be right to bow to the lady, but he smiled at the children, and when she saw him looking so pleasant, the lady said, "That man must be a minister."

My friends, it would be a good thing if all ministers had a smile on their faces. There are more men driven away from churches by sour looks than by anything else. A minister ought to have a clear conscience, and he would wear a pleasant smile. Some of you will say, "Well, Christ was melancholy, and wept over sinners." Ah, but it was love. There is such a thing as a man weeping in his love. Well, the lady said to her little ones, "I want you to follow that gentleman, for I am sure he is a minister." And when he came round again the children went after him, shadowing him through several streets, until by-and-by he turned into an Independent church. The children followed him right in and they brought home a good report. They said they never had such a preacher, although probably they did not understand a word he said. But you know a little pat on the head and a kindly look goes a long way with children. Well, the result was that the mother came and she brought the father. They became converted, and thus, a whole family was brought to Christ by a smile.

We want to believe that the love of Christ is the best thing we can have. If a man wants to buy a horse he goes around till he finds the best horse for his money. You women, if you want to buy a dress, go from one store to another and search till you find the best dress. And it is the universal law of the world over. So if we can show the sinners, by love, that the religion of Jesus Christ is the best thing to have, we can win the world to us. If we can only show that we are full of love and not full of envy and malice and bitterness, everyone can be won to Christ. If the Spirit of love can come upon all of us, so that we can talk to everyone kindly, it will not be long before salvation shall break over us through Christ.

You go into a church that is all aglow with love and into another where there is a lack, and mark the difference. In the latter the people get as far away from the pulpit as possible; and mark the coldness, and see how quickly they get out of the church. Their hearts are cold to one another, and they have no sympathy. But when their hearts are all aglow they crowd round and are genial toward one another, and say, "God bless the sermon," however poor the minister who preaches. The reason that we have so many poor ministers is because we have so few praying people. Look at Joshua. While he was fighting for the Lord, Moses was up on the mountain praying. So we want everyone to pray for their ministers while they are fighting for the Lord. When a man comes to me and grumbles and complains about his minister, I ask him, "Do you ever pray for your minister?" He runs away. It spikes his guns. They do not work with the minister, never think of praying for him. We want to see every man red hot for the Savior, and he will wake up the church. If he had got his heart red hot, sparks will kindle in the little circle, and the whole church will be ablaze. Every soul will be filled with the glory of Christ. There is not a man in all Chicago—I do not care what he is; he may be an atheist, a pantheist, a drunkard, or a gambler—I do not believe that a man's heart is so hard but that God can break it.

Mr. Warner, superintendent of probably one of the largest Sunday schools in the world, had a theory that he would never put a boy out of his school for bad conduct. He argued that if a boy misbehaved himself, it was through bad training at home, and that if he put him out of the school no one would take care of him. Well, this theory was put to the test one day. A teacher came to him and said, "I have a boy in my class that must be taken out; he breaks the rules continually; he swears and uses obscene language; and I cannot do anything with him." Mr. Warner did not care [to put] the boy out, so he sent the teacher back to his class. But the teacher came again and said that unless the boy was taken from his class, he must leave it. Well, he left, and a second teacher was appointed. The second teacher came with the same story and met with the same reply from Mr. Warner. And the teacher resigned. A third teacher was appointed, and he came with the same story as the others. Mr. Warner then thought he would be compelled to turn the boy out at last. One day a few teachers were standing about, and Mr. Warner said, "I will bring this boy up and read his name out in the school, and publicly excommunicate him." Well, a young lady came up and said to him, "I am not doing what I might for Christ; let me have the boy; I will try and save him." But Mr. Warner said, "If these young men cannot do it you will not." But she begged to have him, and Mr. Warner consented. She was a wealthy young lady, and surrounded with all the luxuries of life.

The boy went to her class, and for several Sundays he

behaved himself and broke no rule. But one Sunday he broke loose, and in reply to something she said, spat in her face. She took out her pocket handkerchief and wiped her face, but said nothing. Well, she thought upon a plan, and she said to him, "John"—we will call him John—"John, come home with me." "No," said he, "I won't; I won't be seen on the streets with you." She was fearful of losing him altogether if he went out of the school that day, and she said to him, "Will you let me walk home with you?" "No, I won't," said he. "I won't be seen on the street with you." Then she thought upon another plan. She thought of the "Old Curiosity Shop," and she said, "I won't be at home tomorrow or Tuesday, but if you will come round to the front door on Wednesday morning there will be a little bundle for you." "I don't want it; you may keep your old bundle." She went home, but made up the bundle. She thought that curiosity might make him come.

Wednesday morning arrived, and he got over his mad fit, and he thought he would just like to see what was in this bundle. The little fellow knocked at the door, which was opened, and he told his story. She said, "Yes, here is the bundle." The boy opened it and found a vest, a coat, and other clothing, and a little note written by the young lady, which read something like this:

> Dear Johnnie: Ever since you have been in my class I have prayed for you every morning and evening, that you might be a good boy, and I want you to stay in my class. Do not leave me.

The next morning, before she was up, the servant came to her and said there was a little boy below who wished to see her. She dressed hastily, and went downstairs, and found Johnnie on the sofa weeping. She put her arms around his neck, and he said to her, "My dear teacher, I have not had any peace since I got this note from you. I want you to forgive me." "Won't you let me pray for you to come to Jesus?" And she went down on her knees and prayed. And now, Mr. Warner said, that boy was the best boy in the Sunday school.

And so it was love that broke that boy's heart. May the Lord give us that love in abundance! May we be so full of love that everyone may see that it only prompts us to bring them to heaven!

The text, as presented by Moody, asks the age-old question, "Who is my neighbor?" This issue is a fundamental part of the great commandment to love God first, then love your neighbor as yourself. Such love clearly places a high value on others.

Yet we often misjudge the identity of our neighbor, as the parable clearly shows. Moody masterfully tells how an injured man never received basic care from the very people who were in the businesss of helping. In modern terms, the priest represents the busy pastor, and the Levite a potential deacon. Both are so consumed with the mechanics of the ministry that they completely overlook its true purpose.

Now the Samaritan is the great contradiction. In Moody's thinking he represents the undesirable person we all shun and consider unfit for contact under any circumstance. Yet this same outcast is also the hero, for he clearly demonstrates the essence of the ministry: concern for a neighbor's needs before personal interests.

Moody used this message to attack the petty fighting among various denominations and individuals of his day. Their foolish emphasis on trivial matters caused them to miss the weightier matters of the kingdom. Such a message, to love your neighbor, has never gone out of style.

CHAPTER THREE

The Good Samaritan

You will find my text in part of the twenty-ninth verse of the tenth chapter of Luke, "And who is my neighbor?" We are told that as Christ stood with His disciples, a man, a lawyer, stood up and tempted Him and said, "Master, what shall I do to inherit eternal life?" He asked what he could do to inherit eternal life, what he could do to buy salvation. And the Lord answered his question, "What is written in the Law? How readest thou?" To which the lawyer answered, "Thou shalt love the Lord God with all thy heart, and with all thy soul, and with all thy strength, and with all thy mind, and thy neighbor as thyself." "Thou hast answered right," but who is "thy neighbor"? He drew a vivid picture, which has been told for the last eighteen hundred years, and I do not know anything that brings out more truthfully the wonderful power of the gospel than this story, which we have heard read tonight—the story of the man who went down from Jerusalem to Jericho, and who fell among thieves.

Jerusalem was called the "city of peace." Jericho

41

and the road leading to it were infested with thieves. Probably it had been taken possession of by the worst of Adam's sons. I do not know how far the man got from Jerusalem to Jericho, but the thieves had come out and fallen upon him, and had taken all his money, and stripped him of his clothes, and left him wounded—left him, I suppose, for dead. By-and-by a priest came down the road from Jerusalem. We are told that he came by chance. Perhaps he was going down to dedicate some synagogue, or preach a sermon on some important subject, and had the manuscript in his pocket. As he was going along on the other side he heard a groan, and he turned around and saw the poor fellow lying bleeding on the ground and pitied him. He went up close, took a look at him, and said, "Why, that man's a Jew, he belongs to the seed of Abraham. If I remember aright, I saw him in the synagogue last Sunday. I pity him. But I have too much business, and I cannot attend to him."

He felt a pity for him, and looked on him, and probably wondered why God allowed such men as those thieves to come into the world, and passed by. There are a good many men just like him. They stop to discuss and wonder why sin came into the world, and look upon a wounded man, but do not stop to pick up a poor sinner, forgetting the fact that sin is in the world already, and it has to be rooted out.

But another man came along, a Levite, and he heard the groans. He turned and looked on him with pity, too. He felt compassion for him. He was one of those men that, if we had him here, we should probably make him an elder or a deacon. He looked at him and said, "Poor fellow! He's all covered with blood, he has been badly hurt, he is nearly dead, and they have taken all his money and stripped him naked. Ah, well, I pity him!"

He [wanted] to help him, but he, too, had pressing business, and [he] passed by on the other side. But he had scarcely got out of sight when another came along, riding on a beast. He heard the groans of the wounded man, went over and took a good look at him. The traveler was a Samaritan. When he looked down he saw the man was a Jew. Ah, how the Jews looked down upon the Samaritans. There was a great, high partition wall between the Jews and the Samaritans. The Jews would not allow them in the temple. They would not have any dealings with them. They would not associate with them.

I can see him coming along that road, with his good, benevolent face; and as he passes he hears a groan from this poor fellow. He draws in his beast and pauses to listen. "And he came to where he was." This is the sweetest thing to my mind in the whole story. A good many people would like to help a poor man if he was on the platform, if it cost them no trouble. They want him to come to them. They are afraid to touch the wounded man; he is all bloody, and they will get their hands soiled.

And that was just the way with the priest and the Levite. This poor man, perhaps, had paid half of all his means to help the service of the temple, and might have been a constant worshipper, but they only felt pity for him.

This good Samaritan "came to where he was," and after he saw him he had compassion on him. That word "compassion"—how sweet it sounds! The first thing he did on hearing him cry for water—the hot sun had been pouring down upon his head—was to go and get it from a brook. Then he went and got a bag that he had with him—what we might call a carpetbag or a saddlebag in the west—and poured oil on his wounds. Then he thought, "The poor fellow is weak," and he went and got a little wine. He had been lying so long in the burning sun that he was nearly dead now—he was left half-dead—and the wine revived him. He looked him over, and he saw his wounds that wanted to be bound up. But he had nothing to do this with. I can see him now tearing the lining out of his coat, and with it binding up his wounds. Then he took him up and laid him on his bosom till he revived, and when the poor fellow had strength enough, the good Samaritan put him on his own beast. If the Jew had not been half-dead he would never have allowed him to put his hands on him. He would have treated him with scorn. But he was half-dead, and he could not prevent the good Samaritan treating him kindly and putting him on his beast.

Did you ever stop to think what a strong picture it would have been if the Samaritan had not been able himself to get the man on the beast—if he had had to call for any assistance? Perhaps a man would have come along, and he would have asked him to help him with the wounded man. "What are you?" he might have said. "I am a Samaritan." You are a Samaritan, are you? I cannot help you, I am a Jew."

There is a good deal of that spirit now, just as strong as it was then. When we are trying to get a poor man on the right way, when we are tugging at him to get his face toward Zion, we ask someone to help us, and he says, "I am a Roman Catholic." "Well," you say, "I am a Protestant." So they give no assistance to one another. The same party spirit of old is present today. The Protestants will have nothing to do with the Catholics, the Jews will have nothing to do with the Gentiles. And there was a time—but, thank God, we are getting over it—when a Methodist would not touch a Baptist, or a Presbyterian a Congregationalist; and if we saw a Methodist taking a man out of the ditch, a Baptist would say, "Well, what are you going to do with him?" "Take him to a Methodist church." "Well, I'll have nothing to do with him." A great deal of this has gone by, and the time is coming when, if we are trying to get a man out of the ditch, and they see us tugging at him, and we are so weak that we cannot get him on the beast, they will help him. And that is what Christ wants.

Well, the Samaritan gets him on his beast, and says to

him, "You are very weak; my beast is sure-footed, he will take you to the inn, and I will hold you." He holds him firmly; and God is able to hold everyone He takes out of the pit. I see them going along that road, he holding [the Jew] on, and he gets him to the inn. He gets him there, and he says to the innkeeper, "Here is a wounded man; the thieves have been after him; give him the best attention you can; nothing is too good for him." And I can imagine the good Samaritan as stopping there all night, sitting up with him, and attending to his wants. And the next morning he gets up, and says to the landlord, "I must be off," leaving a little money to pay for what the man has had; "and if that is not enough, I will pay what is necessary when I return from my business in Jericho." This good Samaritan gave this landlord two pence to pay for what he had got, and promised to come again and repay whatever had been spent to take care of the man. And he had given him, besides, all his sympathy and compassion.

And Christ told this story in answer to the lawyer who came to tempt Him, and showed that the Samaritan was the neighbor. Now this story is brought out here to teach the churchgoers this thing: that it is not creeds or doctrines that we want, so much as compassion and sympathy. I have been talking about the qualifications which we require in working for Christ. First night I took "courage," then "love," and last night "faith," and now it is "compassion and sympathy."

If we have not compassion and sympathy our efforts will go for naught. There are hundreds of Christians who work here who do very little because they have not sympathy. If they go to lift up a man, they must put themselves in his place. If you place yourself in sympathy with a man you are trying to do good to, you will soon lift him up.

When at the Hippodrome in New York, a young man came up to me; he looked very sad, his face was troubled.

I asked him what was the matter, and he said, "I am a fugitive from justice. In England, when I was young, my father used to take me into the public house with him, and I learned the habit of drinking, and liquor has become to me like water. A few months ago I was in England, where I was head clerk in a large firm; I was doing well. I had fifty dollars a week. Well, one night I was out, and I had some money of my employers with me, and I got to gambling and lost it. I ran away from England and left a wife and two lovely children. Here I am; I cannot get anything to do; I have no letters of recommendation; and what shall I do?" "Believe in the Lord Jesus Christ," said I. "I cannot become a Christian with that record behind me, there is no hope for me," he replied. "There is hope; seek Jesus, and leave everything behind," I told him. "Well," said he, "I cannot do that until I make restitution." But I kept him to that one thing. He wrote me a letter, and said that the sermon "Ye Must be Born Again," had made a great impression on him. He could not sleep that night, and he finally passed from darkness into light. He came to me, and he said, "I am willing to go back to England and surrender myself, and go into prison, if Christ wants it." I said to him, "Don't do that; but write to your employers and say that if Christ helps you you will make restitution. Live as economically as you can, and be industrious, and you will soon find all well." The man wrote to his employers, and I got a letter from him shortly afterward, and he told me that his wife was coming out to New York. When I was last there I made inquiry about him, and found that he was doing well. He only wanted sympathy—someone to take him by the hand and help him.

I believe that there are not less than ten thousand young men in Chicago who are just waiting for someone to come to them with sympathy. You do not know how far a loving word will go. When I came to this city twenty years ago, I remember I walked up and down the streets trying to find a situation; and I recollect how, when they roughly answered me, their treatment would chill my soul. But when someone would say, "I feel for you; I would like to help you, but I can't; but you will be all right soon," I went away happy and lighthearted. That man's sympathy did me good.

When I first went away from home and to a place some thirteen miles away, it seemed as if I could never be any further away. My brother had gone to live at that town a year and a half before. I recollect, as I walked down the street with him, I was very homesick, and could hardly keep down the tears. My brother said to me, "There's a man here will give you a cent; he gives a cent to every new boy that comes here." I thought that he would be the best man I had ever met. By-and-by he came along, and I thought he was going to pass me. My brother stopped him, thinking, I suppose, I was going to lose the cent, and the old gentleman—he was an old gentleman— looked at me and said, "Why, I have never seen you before: you must be a new boy." "Yes," said my brother, "he has just come." The old man put his trembling hand upon my head, and patted it and told me that I had a Father in heaven, although my earthly father was dead, and he gave me a new cent. I don't know where that cent went to, but the kindly touch of that old man's hand upon my head has been felt by me all these years.

What we want is sympathy from men. There are hundreds of men with hearts full of love, who, if they received but words of sympathy, their hearts would be won to a higher life. But I can imagine men saying, "How are you going to reach them? How are you going to do it? How are you going to get into sympathy with these people?" It is very easily done. Put yourself in their places. There is a young man, a great drunkard; perhaps his father was a drunkard. If you had been surrounded with influences like his, perhaps you would have been a worse drunkard than he is. Well, just put yourself in his place, and go and speak to him lovingly and kindly.

I want to tell you a lesson taught me in Chicago a few years ago. In the months of July and August a great many deaths occurred among children, you all know. I remember I attended a great many funerals; sometimes I would go to two or three funerals a day. I got so used to it that it did not trouble me to see a mother take the last kiss and the last look at her child, and see the coffin lid closed. I got accustomed to it, as in the war we got accustomed to the great battles, and to see the wounded and the dead never troubled us. When I got home one night I heard that one of my Sunday school pupils was dead, and her mother wanted me to come to the house. I went to the poor home, and saw the father drunk. Adelaide had been brought from the river. The mother told me she washed for a living, the father earned no money, and poor Adelaide's work was to get wood for the fire. She had gone to the river that day and seen a piece floating on the water, had stretched out for it, had lost her balance, and fallen in. The poor [mother] was very much distressed. "I would like you to help me, Mr. Moody," she said, "to bury my child. I have no lot; I have no money." Well, I took the measure for the coffin and came away.

I had my little girl with me, and she said, "Papa, suppose we were very, very poor, and Mamma had to work for a living, and I had to get sticks for the fire, and was to fall into the river: would you be very sorry?" This question reached my heart. "Why, my child, it would break my heart to lose you," I said, and I drew her to my bosom. "Papa, do you feel bad for that mother?" she said, and this word woke my sympathy for the woman. And I started and went back to the house and prayed that the Lord might bind up that wounded heart.

When the day came for the funeral I went to Graceland. I had always thought my time too precious to go out there, but I went. The drunken father was there and the poor mother. I bought a lot, the grave was dug, and the child was laid among strangers. There was another funeral coming up, and the corpse was laid near the grave of little Adelaide. And I thought how I would feel if it had been my little girl that I had been laying there among strangers. I went to my Sabbath school thinking this, and suggested that the children should contribute and buy a lot in which we might bury a hundred poor little children. We soon got it, and the papers had scarcely been made out when a lady came and said, "Mr. Moody, my little girl died this morning, let me bury her in the lot you have got for the Sunday school children." The request was granted, and she asked me to go to the lot and say prayers over her child. I went to the grave—it was a beautiful day in June, and I remember asking her what the name of her child was. She said Emma. That was the name of my little girl, and I thought, "What if it had been my own child?" We should put ourselves in the places of others. I could not help shedding a tear. Another woman came shortly after and wanted to put another one into the grave. I asked his name. It was Willie, and it happened to be the name of my little boy—the first two laid there were called by the same names as my two children, and I felt sympathy and compassion for those two women.

If you want to get into sympathy, put yourself into a man's place. Chicago needs Christians whose hearts are full of compassion and sympathy. If we haven't got it, pray that we may have it, so that we may be able to reach those men and women that need kindly words and kindly actions far more than sermons. The mistake is that we have been preaching too much and sympathizing too little. The gospel of Jesus Christ is a gospel of deeds and not of words. May the Spirit of the Lord come upon us this night. May we remember that Christ was moved in compassion for us, and may we, if we find some poor man going down among thieves, or lying wounded and bleeding, look upon him with sympathy, and get below him, and raise him up.

Heaven is the destiny of all who are truly born again. Yet the Bible reveals very little about such a place. The fact that little is said does not make heaven questionable or less desirable.

Moody encountered many who were skeptical about heaven. Yet his faith in the Bible supported his strong belief that such a place existed. Heaven is the place where all departed saints reside. It is the place that fulfills the promise Jesus made when He said He was going to prepare a place for His own (John 14:2).

Throughout this sermon Moody stressed the importance of working for the future and not the present. To be consumed with the treasures of this world would cost the lost person eternal bliss, and the Christian a fruitful life.

The church was never intended to be a place of rest and comfort, but work and toil, always pointing to the fact that the Christian's life is to be spent serving Christ, with heaven as the final place of rest when the work on earth is done.

CHAPTER FOUR

Heaven

Part One

I was on my way to a meeting one night with a friend, and he asked, as we were drawing near the church, "Mr. Moody, what are you going to preach about?" "I am going to preach about heaven," I said. I noticed a scowl passing over his face, and I said, "What makes you look so?" "Why, your subject of heaven. What's the use of talking upon a subject that's all speculation? It's only wasting time on a subject about which you can only speculate." My answer to that friend was, "If the Lord didn't want us to speak about heaven He would never have told us about such a place in the Scriptures, and, as Timothy says, 'All the Scriptures are given by inspiration, and all parts are profitable.'" There's no part of the Word of God that is not profitable, and I believe if men would read more carefully these Scriptures they would think more of heaven.

If we want to get men to fix their hearts and attention upon heaven we must get them to read more about it.

Men who say that heaven is a speculation have not read their Bibles. In the blessed Bible there are allusions scattered all through it. If I were to read to you all the passages on heaven from Genesis to Revelation, it would take me all night and tomorrow to do it. When I took some of the passages lately and showed them to a lady, "Why," said she, "I didn't think there was so much about heaven in the Bible." If I were to go into a foreign land and spend my days there, I would like to know all about it; I would like to read all about it. I would want to know all about its climate, its inhabitants, their customs, their privileges, their government. I would find nothing about that land that would not interest me. Suppose you all were going away to Africa, to Germany, to China, and were going to make one of those places your home, and suppose that I had just come from some of those countries; how eagerly you would listen. I can imagine how the old gray-haired men and the young men and the deaf would crowd around and put up their hands to learn anything about it.

My friends, where are you going to spend eternity? Your life here is very brief. Life is but an inch of time; it is but a span; but a fiber, which will soon be snapped, and you will be ushered into eternity. Where are you going to spend it? If I were to ask you who were going to spend your eternity in heaven to stand up, nearly every one of you would rise. There is not a man here, not one in Chicago, who has not some hope of reaching heaven. Now, if we are going to spend our future there, it becomes us to go to work and find out all about it. I call your attention to this truth: that heaven is just as much a place as Chicago. It is a destination—it is a locality. Some people say there is no heaven. Some men will tell you this earth is all the heaven we have. Queer kind of heaven this. Look at the poverty, the disease in the city; look at the men out of employment walking around our streets, and they say this is heaven. How low a man has [become] when he comes to think in this way. There is a land where the weary are at rest; there is a land where there is peace and joy—where no sorrow dwells. And as we think of it and speak about it, how sweet it looms up before us.

I remember, soon after I got converted, a pantheist got hold of me and just tried to draw me back to the world. Those men who try to get hold of a young convert are the worst set of men. I don't know a worse man than he who tries to pull young Christians down. He is nearer the borders of hell than any man I know. When this man knew I had found Jesus he just tried to pull me down. He tried to argue with me, and I did not know the Bible very well then, and he got the best of me. The only thing to get the best of these atheists, pantheists, or infidels is to have a good knowledge of the Bible. Well, this pantheist told me God was everywhere—in the air, in the sun, in the moon, in the earth, in the stars, but really he meant nowhere. And the next time I went to pray it seemed as if I was not praying anywhere or to anyone.

We have ample evidence in the Bible that there is such a place as heaven, and we have abundant manifestation that His influence from heaven is felt among us. He is not in person among us; only in Spirit. The sun is 95 million miles from the earth, yet we feel its rays. In Second Chronicles we read, "If my people, which are called by my name, shall humble themselves, and pray, and seek my face, and turn from their wicked ways; then will I hear from heaven and forgive their sin, and will heal their land." Here is one reference, and when it is read a great many people might ask, "How far away is heaven? Can you tell us that?" I don't know how far away it is, but there is one thing I can tell you: He can hear prayer as soon as the words are uttered. There has not been a prayer said that He has not heard; not a tear shed that

He has not seen. We don't want to learn the distance. What we want to know is that God is there, and Scripture tells us that.

Turn to First Kings and we read, "And hearken thou to the supplication of Thy servant and of Thy people Israel, when they shall pray toward this place, and hear Thou in heaven, Thy dwelling place, and when Thou hearest forgive." Now, it is clearly taught in the word of God that the Father dwells there. It is His dwelling place, and in Acts we see that Jesus is there too. "But he being full of the Holy Ghost looked up steadfastly into heaven and saw the glory of God, and Jesus standing on the right hand of God," and by the eye of faith we can see them there tonight too. And by faith we shall be brought into His presence, and we shall be satisfied when we gaze upon Him. Stephen, when he was surrounded by the howling multitude, saw the Son of man there, and when Jesus looked down upon earth and saw this first martyr in the midst of his persecution, He looked down and gave him a welcome. We'll see Him by-and-by.

It is not the jasper streets and golden gates that attract us to heaven. What are your golden palaces on earth— what is that that makes them so sweet? Is it the presence of some loving wife or fond children? Let them be taken away and the charm of your home is gone. And so it is Christ that is the charm of heaven to the Christian. Yes, we shall see Him there. How sweet the thought that we shall dwell with Him forever, and shall see the nails in His hands and in His feet which He received for us.

I read a little story not long since which went to my heart. A mother was on the point of death, and the child was taken away from her in case it would annoy her. [The child] was crying continually to be taken to [her] mother and teased the neighbors. By-and-by the mother died, and the neighbors thought it was better to bury the mother without letting the child see her dead face. They thought the sight of the dead mother would not do the child any good, and so they kept her away. When the mother was buried and the child was taken back to the house, the first thing she did was to run into her mother's sitting room and look all round it, and from there to the bedroom, but no mother was there. And she went all over the house crying, "Mother, Mother!" but the child could not find her, and then said to the neighbor, "Take me back, I don't want to stay here if I cannot see my mother." It wasn't the home that made it so sweet to the child. It was the presence of the mother. And so it is not heaven that is alone attractive to us; it is the knowledge that Jesus, our leader, our brother, our Lord, is there.

And the spirits of loved ones, whose bodies we have laid in the earth, will be there. We shall be in good company there. When we reach that land we shall meet all the Christians who have gone before us. We are told in Matthew, too, that we shall meet angels there. "Take heed lest ye despise not one of these little ones, for I say unto you that in heaven their angels do always behold the face of my Father which is in heaven." Yes, the angels are there, and we shall see them when we get home.

He is there, and where He is His disciples shall be, for He has said, "I go and prepare a mansion for you, that wheresoever I am there ye may be also." I believe that when we die the spirit leaves the body and goes to the mansion above, and by-and-by the body will be resurrected and it shall see Jesus. Very often people come to me and say, "Mr. Moody, do you think we shall know each other in heaven?" Very often it is a mother who has lost a dear child, and who wishes to see it again. Sometimes it is a child who has lost a mother, a father, and who wants to recognize them in heaven. There is just one verse in Scripture in answer to this, and that is, "We shall be satisfied." It is all I want to know. My brother who went up there the other day I shall see, because I will be satisfied. We will see all those we loved on earth up there, and if we loved them here we will love them ten thousand times more when we meet them there.

Another thought. In the tenth chapter of Luke we are told our names are written there if we are Christians. Christ just called His disciples up and paired them off and sent them out to preach the gospel. Two of us—Mr. Sankey and myself—going about and preaching the gospel is nothing new. You will find them away back eighteen hundred years ago going off two by two, like brothers Bliss and Whittle, and brothers Needham and Morehouse, to different towns and villages. They had gone out, and there had been great revivals in all the cities, towns, and villages they had entered. Everywhere they had met with the greatest success. Even the very devils were subject to them. Disease had fled before them. When they met a lame man they said to him, "You don't want to be lame any longer," and he walked. When they met a blind man they but told him to open his eyes, and behold he could see. And they came to Christ and rejoiced over their great success, and He said to them, "I will give you something to rejoice over. Rejoice that your names are written in heaven." Now, there are a great many people who do not believe in such an assurance as this: "Rejoice, because your names are written in heaven." How are you going to rejoice if your names are not written there?

While speaking about this some time ago, a man told me we were preaching a very ridiculous doctrine when we preached this doctrine of assurance. I ask you in all candor, what are you going to do with this assurance if we don't preach it? It is stated that our names are written there, blotted out of the Book of Death and transferred to the Book of Life.

I was with a friend while in Europe—she is in this hall tonight. On one occasion we were traveling from London to Liverpool, and the question was put as to where we would stop. We said we would go to the Northwestern at Lime Street, as that was the hotel where Americans generally stopped. When we got there the house was full, could not let us in. Every room was engaged. But this friend said, "I am going to stay here. I engaged a room ahead. I sent a telegram on."

My friends, that is just what the Christians are doing—sending their names in ahead. They are sending a message up saying, "Lord Jesus, I want one of those mansions you are preparing; I want to be there." That's what they're doing. And every man and woman here who wants one, if you have not already got one, had better make up [your] mind. Send your names up now. I would rather a thousand times have my name written in the Lamb's Book than have all the wealth of the world rolling at my feet.

A man may get station in this world, but it will fade away; he may get wealth, but it will prove a bubble. "What shall it profit a man if he gain the whole world and lose his own soul?" It is a solemn question, and let it go around the hall tonight: "Is my name written in the Book of Life?" I can imagine that man down there saying, "Yes; I belong to the Presbyterian church; my name's on the church's books." It may be, but God keeps His books in a different fashion than that in which the church records of this city are kept. You may belong to a good many churches; you may be an elder or a deacon and be a bright light in your church, and yet you may not have your name written in the Book of Life. Judas was one of the twelve, and yet he hadn't his name written in the Book of Life. Satan was among the elect—he dwelt among the angels, and yet he was cast from the high hallelujahs. Is your name written in the Book of Life?

A man told me while speaking upon this subject, "That is all nonsense you are speaking." And a good many men here are of the same opinion; but I would like them to turn to Daniel, twelfth chapter, "And there shall be a time of trouble, such as never was since there was a nation, even to that same time: and at that time thy people shall be delivered, every one that shall be found written in the book." Everyone shall be delivered whose names shall be found written in the book. And we find Paul, in the letters which he wrote to the Philippians, addressing them as those "dear yokefellows, whose names were written in the Book of Life." If it is not our privilege to know that our names are written in the Book of Life, here is Paul sending greeting to his yokefellows, "whose names were written in the book." Let us not be deceived in this. We see it too plainly throughout the Holy Word. In the chapter of Revelation which we have just read, we have three different passages referring to it, and in the twenty-seventh verse, almost the last words in the Scriptures, we read, "And there shall in no wise enter into it anything that defileth, neither whatsoever worketh abomination or maketh a lie: but they which are written in the Lamb's Book of Life." My friends, you will never see the city unless your name is written in that Book of Life. It is a solemn truth. Let it go home to everyone and sink into the hearts of all here tonight. Don't build your hopes on a false foundation; don't build your hopes on an empty profession. Be sure your name is written there. And the next thing after your own names are written there is to see that the names of the children God has given you are recorded there. Let the fathers and mothers assembled tonight hear this and take it to their hearts. See that your children's names are there. Ask your conscience if the name of your John, your Willie, your Mary, your Alice—ask yourselves whether their names are recorded in the Book of Life. If not, make it the business of your life, rather than to pile up wealth for them, make it the one object of your existence to secure for them eternal life rather than to pave the way to their death and ruin.

I read some time ago of a mother in an eastern city

who was stricken with consumption. At her dying hour she requested her husband to bring the children to her. The oldest one was brought first to her, and she laid her hand on his head and gave him her blessing and dying message. The next one was brought, and she gave him the same; and one after another came to her bedside until the little infant was brought in. She took it and pressed it to her bosom, and the people in the room, fearing that she was straining her strength, took the child away from her. As this was done she turned to the husband and said, "I charge you, sir, bring all those children home with you." And so God charges us. The promise is to ourselves and to our children. We can have our names written there, and then by the grace of God we can call our children to us and know that their names are also recorded there. That great roll is being called, and those bearing the names are summoned every day—every hour; that great roll is being called tonight, and if your name were shouted could you answer with joy? You have heard of a soldier who fell in our war. While he was dying, he was heard to cry, "Here! here!" Some of his comrades went up to him thinking he wanted water, but he said, "They are calling the roll of heaven, and I am answering." And in a faint voice he whispered, "Here!" and passed away to heaven.

If that roll was called tonight would you be ready to answer: "Here"? I am afraid not. Let us wake up. May every child of God wake up tonight. There is work to do. Fathers and mothers, look to your children. If I could only speak to one class, I would preach to parents, and try to show them the great responsibility that rests upon them.

There is a man living on the bank of the Mississippi River. The world calls him rich, but if he could call back his first-born son he would give up all his wealth. The boy was brought home one day unconscious. When the doctor examined him, he turned to the father who stood at the bedside and said, "There is no hope." "What?" exclaimed the father, "Is it possible my boy has got to die?" "There is no hope," replied the doctor. "Will he not come to?" asked the father. "He may resume consciousness, but he cannot live." "Try all your skill, doctor. I don't want my boy to die." By-and-by the boy regained a glimmering of consciousness, and when he was told that his death was approaching, he said to his father, "Won't you pray for my lost soul, Father? You have never prayed for me." The old man only wept. It was true. During the seventeen years that God had given him his boy, he had never spent an hour in prayer for his soul, but the object of his life had been to accumulate wealth for that first-born. Am I speaking to a prayerless father or mother tonight? Settle the question of your soul's salvation, and pray for the son or daughter God has given you.

But I have another anecdote to tell. It was Ralph Wallace who told me of this one. A certain gentleman had been a member of the Presbyterian church. His little boy was sick. When he went home, his wife was weeping, and she said, "Our boy is dying. He has had a change for the worse. I wish you would go in and see him." The father went into the room and placed his hand on the brow of his dying boy, and [he] could feel that the cold, damp sweat was gathering there; that the cold, icy hand of death was feeling for the chords of life. "Do you know, my boy, that you are dying?" asked the father. "Am I? Is this death? Do you really think I am dying?" "Yes, my son, your end on earth is near." "And will I be with Jesus tonight, Father?" "Yes, you will be with the Savior." "Father, don't you weep, for when I get there I will go right straight to Jesus and tell Him that you have been trying all my life to lead me to Him."

God has given me two little children, and ever since I can remember I have directed them to Christ, and I would rather lead them to Jesus than give them the wealth of the world. If you have got a child, go and point the way. I challenge any man to speak of heaven without speaking of children, "for of such is the kingdom of heaven." Fathers and mothers and professed Christians ignore this sometimes. They go along themselves and never try to get any to heaven with them. Let us see to this at once, and let us pray that there may be many names written in the Lamb's Book of Life tonight.

Part Two

You who were here last night remember that the subject upon which I spoke was "Heaven, and Who Were There." We tried to prove from Scripture that God the Father, and Christ the Son, and angels, and redeemed saints who have gone up from earth are there, and that if we have been born of God our names are recorded there.

Now I will commence tonight right where I left off last night, and the next thought upon the subject that presents itself is: "Are we laying our treasures there?" If we are living as God would have us live, we are doing this. There are a great many people who forget that there are eleven commandments. They think there are only ten. The eleventh commandment is, "Lay up for yourselves treasures in heaven." How many of us remember—ah! How people in Chicago forget the words of the Lord now in His wonderful Sermon on the Mount: "Lay not up for yourselves treasures upon earth, where moth and rust doth corrupt, and where thieves break through and steal; but lay up for yourselves treasures in heaven, where neither moth nor rust doth corrupt, and where thieves do not break through nor steal."

How few of our people pay any heed to these words? That's why there are so many broken hearts among us; that's why so many men and women are disappointed and going through the streets with shattered hopes; it's because they have not been laying up treasures in heaven. They pile up treasures on earth, and some calamity comes upon them and sweeps all away. The Chicago fire burned up a good many of these treasures. A great number of people put their treasures in banks, which dissolve, and away they go. Some have put their treasures in railway shares which have all disappeared like a vapor; and that is why so many are brokenhearted today, and in great distress, and do not know what is before them. If they had taken heed of the words of this commandment, this thing would not have happened to them. "Lay up your treasures in heaven." It doesn't take long in conversation with a man to find out where his heart is. Wherever it is, there is his treasure. Go to a political man and talk to him about Hayes and Wheeler or Tilden or Hendricks on any political question, and how his heart gets ablaze and his eye sparkles. His treasure is in politics. Go talk to a man who loves the theater about a new play, and see how his eye glistens. His heart is set upon pleasure—upon the world. And yet [there is] another class whose heart is set on business: go and talk to [a businessman] about some new speculation and show him where he can make a few thousand dollars, and you will soon tell where his treasure lies. But talk about heaven and all interest is lost. I could not help that thought coming to me last night, when I saw before me some dozing—some almost asleep, as if they thought I was talking about a myth; and others were sitting with eyes aglow, and all attention when I mentioned heaven. Ah! They expected to go there and were glad to hear about it.

Some men think it is too far away to lay up their treasures. I was talking to a businessman before the fire about laying up treasures in heaven, and he said, "I like to have my treasure where I can see it." And that is the way with a great many people—they like to have their treasures here so they can see them. It is a great mistake.

People go on accumulating what they must leave behind them. How many here do not devote five minutes to anything else than money-making? It is money, money, money, and if they get it they are satisfied. You will see occasionally in the newspapers accounts of men dying who are worth so many millions. It is a great mistake. He cannot take it with him. If it is in business, it isn't his. If it is in banks, it isn't his. If in real estate, he cannot take it. It isn't his. Now, ask yourselves tonight, "Where is my treasure? Is my heart set upon things down here?" If it is set upon wealth it will by-and-by take to itself wings and fly away. Oh, think of this. If your heart is set upon pleasure, it will melt away; if your heart is set upon station or reputation, some tongue may blast it in a moment, and it is gone. If your hopes and heart are set upon some loved wife or dear children, whom you have set up in your hearts as an idol in place of your God, death may come and snatch your god from your life. It is wrong to set up anything, however dear to us, in the place of our God. And so it is wrong "to lay up treasures for yourselves upon earth."

Now, are you—are the people of Chicago heeding this commandment? Ask yourselves this as you are passing through the street tomorrow: "How many of the people of this city are obeying this commandment: 'Lay up for yourselves treasures in heaven' ?"

I remember before the Chicago fire hearing of a minister coming up to see his son. He found him completely absorbed in real estate. You remember before the fire how everyone was mad about real estate. It was a mania with all of us. If we could get a corner lot, no matter whether we threw ourselves in debt, or smothered it with mortgages, we were confident that in time, when prices went up, we would make our fortune. This minister came up, and when he saw his son he tried to talk about his soul, but it was no use. Real estate was there. He talked about real estate in the morning, in the afternoon, and [at] night. No use of trying to talk of heaven to him. His only heaven was real estate. The son had a boy in his store, but he being absent the father was left to mind the business one day. When a customer came in and started upon the subject of real estate, it was not long before the minister stepped off and was speaking to the customer about his soul, and telling him he would rather have a corner lot in the New Jerusalem than all the corner lots in Chicago. And the people used to say that no real estate could be sold when the father was around. The trouble was that the son had real estate in his heart—that was his god—and his father had in his heart treasures in heaven. If we have anything in our hearts which we put up as our god, let us ask Him to come to us and take it away from us.

I remember when I went to California just to try and get a few souls saved on the Pacific coast. I went into a school there and asked, "Have you got someone who can write a plain hand?" "Yes." Well, we got up [to] the blackboard, and the lesson upon it proved to be the very text we have tonight, "Lay up for yourselves treasures in heaven." And I said, "Suppose we write upon that board some of the earthly treasures? And we will begin with 'gold.'" The teacher readily put down gold, and they all comprehended it; for all had run to that country in the hope of finding it. "Well, we will put down 'houses' next, and then 'land.' Next we will put down 'fast horses.'" They all understood what fast horses were—they knew a good deal more about fast horses than they knew about the kingdom of God. Some of them, I think, actually made fast horses serve as gods. "Next we will put down 'tobacco.'" The teacher seemed to shrink at this. "Put it down," said I, "many a man thinks more of tobacco than he does of God. Well, then, we will put down 'rum.'" He objected to this—didn't like to put it down at all. "Down with it. Many a man will sell his reputation, will sell his home, his wife, children, everything he has. It is the god of some men." Many here in Chicago will sell their present and their eternal welfare for it.

"Now," said I, "suppose we put down some of the heavenly treasures. Put down 'Jesus' to head the list, then 'heaven,' then 'river of life,' then 'crown of glory,' " and went on till the column was filled, and just drew a line and showed the heavenly and the earthly things in contrast. My friends, they could not stand comparison. If a man just does that, he cannot but see the superiority of the heavenly over the earthly treasures.

Well, it turned out that the teacher was not a Christian. He had gone to California on the usual hunt—gold; and when he saw the two columns placed side by side, the excellence of the one over the other was irresistible, and he was the first soul God gave me on that Pacific coast. He accepted Christ, and that man came to the station when I was coming away and blessed me for coming to that place.

Those of you who do not lay your treasures up in heaven will be sure to be disappointed. You cannot find a man who has devoted his life to the treasures of this life—not one in the wide, wide world—but [he] has been disappointed. Something arises in life to sweep all away, or the amount of joy which they expect to obtain from their riches falls short of their anticipations. If men center their affections on heaven they will have no disappointment; all is joy and comfort from that source, and the whole current of their lives will be drifting toward heaven.

Someone has heard of a farmer who, when someone— an agent—called upon him to give something for the Christian Commission, promptly drew a check for ten thousand dollars. He wanted the agent to have dinner with him, and after they had dined the farmer took the man out on the veranda and pointed to the rich lands sweeping far away, laden with rich products. "Look over these lands," said the farmer. "They are all mine." He took him to the pasture and showed the agent the choice stock, the fine horses he had, and then pointed to a little town, and then to a large hall where he lived, saying, "They are all mine. I came here as a poor boy, and I have earned all that you see." When he got through my friend asked him, "Well, what have you got up yonder?" "Where?" replied the farmer, who evidently knew where my friend meant. "What have you got in heaven?" "Well," said the farmer, "I haven't anything there." "What?" replied my friend, "You, a man of your discretion, wisdom, business ability, have made no provision for your future?" He hadn't, and in a few weeks he died—a rich man here and a beggar in eternity. A man may be wise in the eyes of the world to pursue this course, but he is a fool in the sight of God. Wealth to most men proves nothing more or less than a great rock upon which his eternity is wrecked.

A great many Christians wonder how it is they don't get on better—how it is that they don't get on. It is because [they] have got [their] hearts on things down here. When they look toward heaven they don't have a love for the world. [They] are then living for another world. We are pilgrims and strangers upon the earth. It is easy to have love for God when we have our treasures there. The reason, then, why so many of us do not grow in Christianity is because we have our treasures here.

Mr. Morehouse told me he was looking down the harbor of Liverpool one day, when he saw a vessel coming up, and she was being towed up by a tug. The vessel was sunk in the water nearly to her edge, and he wondered it did not sink altogether. Upon inquiry he found that it was loaded with lumber and that it was waterlogged. Another vessel came up, her sails set, no tug assisting her, and she soon darted past the waterlogged vessel. And so it is with some Christians. They are waterlogged. They may belong to a church, and if they find anything in the church disagreeing with them they won't go back. They want the whole church to come out and look for them, and tow them in. If the church doesn't, they think they are not getting the attention due them. When men go up in balloons they take bags of sand with them, and when they want to rise higher they throw them out. There are a great many Christians who have got too many bags of sand, and to rise they [need] to throw some out. Look at the poor men here in the city—the rich Christians can relieve themselves by giving some of their bags of sand to them. A great many Christians would feel much better it they relieved themselves of their bags of sand. "He that giveth to the poor lendeth to the Lord," and if you want to be rich in eternity, just give to the poor with your heart, and the Lord will bless not only you, but all connected with you.

The next thing is our rest in heaven! A great many people have got a false idea about the church. They have got an idea that the church is a place to rest in. Instead of thinking that it is a place of work, they turn it into a resting place. To get into a nicely cushioned pew, and contribute to charities, listen to the minister, and do their share to keep the church out of bankruptcy, is all they want. The idea of work for them—actual work in the church—never enters their mind. In Hebrews we see the words, "There is a rest for the people of God." We have got all eternity to rest in. Here is the place for work; we must work till Jesus comes. This is the place of toil— eternity of repose. "Blessed are they that die in the Lord, for their works do follow them." Let us do the work that God gives us today. Don't think that you have to rest in the world where God sent His Son who was murdered.

I remember hearing a man who had worked successfully for the Lord complaining that he didn't have the success he used to, and one night he threw himself on his bed sick of life and wanting to die. While in this state of mind he dreamed that he was dead and that he had ascended to heaven. And as he was walking down the crystal pavement of paradise he saw all at once three friends in a chariot, and when the chariot came opposite to where he was one of them stepped out and came to him. He noticed that His face was illuminated with a heavenly radiance, and He came to this man and took him to the battlements of heaven. "Look down," said He; "what do you see?" "I see the dark world," replied the dreamer. "Look down again, and tell me what you see." "I see men walking blindfolded over bridges, and below them are bottomless pits," was the dreamer's reply. "Will you prepare to stay here, or go back to earth and tell those men of their danger—tell them of the bottomless pits over which they walk?" At this the man awoke from his sleep and said he didn't want to die anymore. He just wanted to remain down here and warn his fellow men [of] the dangers which surrounded them.

When we turn a soul to Christ we do not know what will turn up—what will be the result of it. It may be the means of saving a million souls. The one man may convert another man, and those two may convert a hundred, and that hundred may convert a thousand, and the current keeps widening and widening and deepening and deepening, and as time rolls on the fruit will ripen which you have gathered for God. It is a great privilege, my friends, to work for God.

I want to call your attention to the eleventh chapter of Hebrews. After Paul mentions Jacob and Isaac and Enoch, he says, "These all died in faith, not having received the promises, but having seen them afar off, and were persuaded of them, and embraced them, and confessed that they were strangers and pilgrims on the earth." Are the Christians of Chicago living like pilgrims and strangers, and by their faith do they show "that they seek another country"; do they show by their fruits and their deeds that they are pilgrims and strangers here? When I get into a man's mind the beauties of that country beyond the grave, it looks as if his only thought was

70

for it. We are to be pilgrims and strangers passing through this world on our way to a better land. The moment Abraham by faith got sight of that land, he declared himself a pilgrim and a stranger. This earth had no charm for him then. Lot might go down to that city of Sodom or Gomorrah, and that city might be burned up. We might fix our affections on this city. Chicago has been burned twice, and it will be burned again—this whole world shall pass away with all its boasted riches and glory, and where shall we be then? If we build our hopes here we shall be disappointed; if we build our hopes upon that foundation whose builder and maker is God, we shall not be disappointed. We are told in Matthew to set our affections on things above, and that "there shall be joy in heaven over one sinner that repenteth."

There are rumors of war in Europe, and if war were declared it would probably excite the whole civilized world. Trade would be affected, and relations of all kinds. I don't know whether it would excite heaven at all. If the President of the United States issued a proclamation, I don't know whether it would be noticed in heaven or not, but the papers would speak of it, the people would be excited, and great changes might take place over it. If Queen Victoria died, telegrams would go all over the world, newspapers would speak of it, the whole world would be excited—I don't know if it would be noticed in heaven at all. But if that girl there should repent there would be joy in heaven. Just think of it—think of a little girl, of a little girl being the cause of joy in heaven. I don't think the papers would record it—they would never notice it. There would be no headline in the morning telling the people that there had been joy in heaven over the repentance of a little girl in the tabernacle. "There is joy over one sinner that repenteth." I have been wondering who it is that rejoiced in heaven when He brought back that lost sheep. We are told that there is joy in the presence of the angels; but who else is it that rejoices? It may be that I am going a little too far, but I think that I have a right to believe that the redeemed saints who have gone up from earth may be led to rejoice when they hear in heaven of the conversion of some living ones here.

Perhaps while I am speaking, some loving mother may be looking over the battlements of heaven on her boy in the gallery yonder, and it may be that while she was on earth she prayed earnestly and constantly, and when she got there she pleaded at the throne for mercy to her son. It may be that as she is watching some angel will carry the news to her of that boy's conversion and take his name there to be recorded in the Book of Life. Perhaps that mother and the Lord Jesus Christ will rejoice over that son, or it may be some daughter. Perhaps it is some child who is looking from that country down to her mother in this hall, and when the news of her acceptance of salvation reaches that little child she will strike her golden harp and shout, "Mother, Mother is coming!" While I was touching on this topic in Manchester I remember a man getting up and shouting, "Oh, Mother, I am coming!" The mother had been fruitless in her endeavors to convert that man while on earth, but her intercession there and the influence of her prayers here touched his heart and he decided.

I remember in the Exposition building in Dublin, while I was speaking about heaven, I said something to the effect that "perhaps at this moment a mother is looking down from heaven upon her daughter here tonight," and I pointed down to a young lady in the audience. Next morning I received this letter:

On Wednesday when you were speaking of heaven you said, "It may be this moment there is a mother looking down from heaven expecting the salvation of her child who is here." You were apparently looking at the very spot where my child was sitting. My heart said, "That is *my* child. That is *her* mother." Tears sprang to my eyes. I bowed my head and prayed, "Lord, direct that word to my darling child's heart; Lord, save my child." I was then anxious till the close of the meeting, when I went to her. She was bathed in tears. She rose, put her arms round me, and kissed me. When walking down to you she told me it was that same remark (about the mother looking down from heaven) that found the way home to her, and asked me, "Papa, what can I do for Jesus?"

May the Spirit of God bring hundreds to the cross of Christ tonight.

The significance of the blood sacrifice began in Eden with the death of several animals to provide clothing for Adam and Eve after they disobeyed God. From that time up to the death of Christ, blood played an important role in biblical history.

The sin of Adam passed on the curse of death to all humanity. Cain and Abel were the first people to show the right and wrong approach to pleasing God in presenting offerings to Him: Abel's blood sacrifice was acceptable; Cain's produce offering was not.

The importance of blood is clearly demonstrated by the story of Abraham. The command for him to sacrifice his son was the first clear picture of what God was later going to do with His Son for the benefit of the world. The blood of Christ made it possible for all individuals to be saved. The blood washed the sinner clean, paying the debt that no one could pay to God.

As Moody described the death of Christ, he made it clear that such a payment was of the greatest value with eternal dividends. All that is required is faith in Christ for the remission of sin. By trusting Christ the sinner finds eternal life and happiness.

CHAPTER FIVE

The Precious Blood

Part One

The subject tonight will be "The Precious Blood." I want to call your attention first to the second chapter and sixteenth verse of Genesis, "And the LORD God commanded the man, saying, Of every tree of the garden thou mayest freely eat: But of the tree of the knowledge of good and evil, thou shalt not eat of it: for in the day that thou eatest thereof thou shalt surely die." There cannot be a law without a penalty. There is not a law in our land but has a penalty attached to it. If our legislative representatives or members of Congress were to make a law and have no penalty appended to it, it would be worthless. We might make a law forbidding men to steal, but if we had no penalty to that law I don't think we could [walk] home without having our watches stolen from us. We could not live without law, and God put Adam into the garden under a law, attached to which was a penalty. Well, we know how he disobeyed and how he fell, and so the penalty of death came upon him. Many people stumble over this. I used to wonder how it was that the penalty of death fell upon him when he lived, I think, some nine hundred and ninety-nine years after he broke the law; but when I understood my Bible better, I learned that it was death to the soul—not physical death, but spiritual death. When God came to seek him in the garden, we are told that he hid himself; he was ashamed of his iniquity—just like hundreds of his sons in Chicago; and then we find Him dealing with Adam by showing him grace. This was the very first thing He did.

A great many people think God was very severe in His treatment of Adam; but whenever the offense was committed, whenever the law was broken, He showed mercy, showed grace; and by this grace a way of escape was presented to them. Ah, that little hymn expresses it: "Grace, friend, contrived a way," by which Adam could regain the life he had forfeited. And so we read that the Lord made "coats of skin" to clothe them before He drove them out of paradise. They received grace before, as we see in the twenty-fourth verse: "He drove out the man, and He placed at the east end of the Garden of Eden cherubims and a flaming sword, which turned every way to keep the way of the tree of life." There's grace and government: and from that day till the present God has been dealing with us in that way.

He rides, we may say, in a chariot with two wheels— one grace and the other government. We can see in this world how it would be if we had no government. There would be no living in it. Adam broke the divine law, and so he had to suffer the penalty; but He gave him grace to be redeemed by. He showed Adam and Eve grace by killing the animals and then covering their nakedness with coats made from the skins. I can imagine Adam's turning to Eve and saying, "Well, in spite of what we've done, God loves us after all. He has clothed us; He has given us grace for our sin." And here we find the first glimpse of the doctrine of substitution—the substitution of the just for the unjust; the great doctrine of atonement and sub-stitution foreshadowed in Genesis.

Then, as we go on, we find the story of Cain and Abel, and we are told that "in process of time it came to pass that Cain brought of the fruit of the ground an offering unto the Lord. And Abel, he also brought of the firstlings of his flock, and of the fat thereof; and the Lord had re-spect unto Abel and to his offering; but unto Cain and his offering He had not respect. And Cain was very wroth and his countenance fell." Now we find that Cain brought a bloodless sacrifice—"he brought of the fruit of the ground"—and Abel brought a bleeding lamb. Right on the morning of grace we see here that God had marked a way for men to come to Him, and that way was the way that Abel took, and Cain came to God with a sac-rifice of his own, in his own way. So we find men and women in the churches of today coming to God with a sacrifice, not in God's way, but in their own—coming with their own good deeds, or their works, or their righ-teousness, and ignoring the Lamb altogether, ignoring the blood completely. They don't want to come that way; they want to come in their own fashion. Cain, perhaps, reasoned that he didn't see why the products of the earth, why the fruit, shouldn't be as acceptable to God as a bleeding lamb. He didn't like a bleeding lamb, and so he brought his fruit. Now we don't know how there was any difference between those two boys. Both must have been brought up in the same way; both came from the same parents, yet we find in the offering there was a dif-ference between them. One came with the blood, and the other without the blood, and the one with the blood had the acceptable sacrifice to God.

We pass over to the second dispensation—to the eighth chapter of Genesis—where we find Noah coming out of the ark and putting blood between him and his sins. "And Noah builded an altar unto the LORD; and took of every clean beast and of every clean fowl, and offered burnt offerings on the altar." God had Noah bring those animals clear through the Flood so that he could offer them as a sacrifice when he came from the ark. He took a couple of each kind into the ark, and when he came out [he made] a blood offering the very first thing. He was a man of God; he walked in the fear of the Lord, and so he made the offering of blood. The first thing in the first dispensation we see is blood, and the first thing in the second dispensation is blood.

In the twenty-second chapter of Genesis we find the story of Abraham and his only son, Isaac. Abraham was a follower of God, a man who loved and feared God, and He commanded him to make a blood sacrifice. We read in this chapter that He commanded Abraham to make the sacrifice of his only son. And we read that the next morning the old man saddled his ass and started. He didn't tell his wife anything about it. If he had she would likely have persuaded him to remain where he was. But he had heard the voice of God, and he obeyed the command; he had heard God's wish, and he was going to do it.

So, early in the morning—he didn't wait till ten or twelve o'clock but went early in the morning—he takes two of his young men with him and his son, Isaac, and you can see him starting out on the three days' journey. They have the wood and the fire, for he is going to worship his God. As he goes on he looks at his boy and says, "It is a strange commandment that God has given. I love this boy dearly. I don't understand it; but I know it's all right, for the Judge of all the earth makes no mistakes." An order from the Judge of heaven is enough for him.

The first night comes, and their little camp is made, and Isaac is asleep. But the old man doesn't sleep. He looks into his [son's] face sadly and says, "I will have no boy soon; I shall never see him on earth again; but I must obey God." I can see him marching on the next day, and you might have seen him drying his tears as he glanced upon that only son and thought upon what he had been called upon to do. The second night comes; tomorrow is the day for the sacrifice. What a night that must have been to Abraham. "Tomorrow," he says sadly, "I must take the life of that boy—my only son, dearer to me than my life—dearer to me than anything on earth."

And the third day comes, and as they go along they see the mountain in the distance; then he says to the young men, "You stay here with the beasts." He takes the wood and the fire, and along with his boy prepares to ascend Mount Moriah, from which could be seen the spot where a few hundred years later the Son of man was offered up. As they ascend the mountain Isaac says, "There's the wood and the fire, Father, but where's the sacrifice?"— thus showing that the boy knows nothing of what is in store. How the question must sink down into the old man's heart. And he answers, "The Lord will provide a sacrifice." It is not time to tell him, and they go on until they come to the place appointed by God, and build the altar, and lay the wood upon it.

Everything is ready, and I can just imagine the old man taking the boy by the hand, and, leading him to a rock, sitting down there, and telling him how God had called upon him to come out of his native land; how God had been in communion with him for fifty years; what God had done for him. "And now," he says, "my boy, when I was in my bed three nights ago, God came to me with a strange message, in which He told me to offer my child as a sacrifice. I love you, my son, but God has told me to do this, and I must obey Him. So let us both go down on our knees and pray to Him." After they have sent up a petition to God, Abraham lays him on the altar and kisses him for the last time. He lifts the knife to drive it into his son's heart, when all at once he hears a voice: "Abraham, Abraham, spare thine only son."

Ah, there was no voice heard on Calvary to save the Son of man. God showed mercy to the son of Abraham.

You fathers and mothers, just picture to yourselves how you would suffer if you had to sacrifice your only son; and think what it must have [cost] God to give up His only Son. We are told that Abraham was glad. The manifestations of Abraham's faith so pleased God that He showed him the grace of heaven, and lifted the curtain of time to let him look down into the future to see the Son of God offered, bearing the sins of the world. From the peak of this very mountain might have been seen the very spot where died the Savior of the world.

We find Abel the first man who went to heaven, and he went by way of blood, and we find it in all the worships of God from the earliest times. Mr. Sankey sings solos upon the redeeming blood. I can imagine when Abel got there how he sang the song of redemption. How the angels gathered around him and listened to that song; it was the first time they had ever heard that song; but six thousand years have gone, and there's a great chorus of the saints redeemed by the atoning blood. The first man that went to heaven went by the way of blood, and the last man who passes through those pearly gates must go the same way. We find not only Abel and Abraham and Isaac and Jacob, but all of them, went there through an atonement.

Now, we find in the twelfth chapter and second verse of Exodus—the most important chapter in the Word of God: "This month shall be unto you the beginning of months: it shall be the first month of the year to you." And then in the fourth verse, "And if the household be too little for the lamb, let him and his neighbor next unto his house take it according to the number of the souls; every man according to his eating shall make your count for the lamb." Now it doesn't say "if the lamb be too small for the household," but "if the household be too little for the lamb." You may have some pretty large households; your houses may be too small for them, but Christ has plenty of room. We don't start from the cradle to heaven, but from the cross. That's where eternal life begins—when we come to Calvary; when we come to Christ and get grace. We don't come to heaven when we are born into the natural world, but into the spiritual world. That's where we date our spiritual lives from. Before that our lives are a blank so far as grace is concerned.

Adam dated from the time of the [Fall], and Noah when he came from the ark dated from the blood offering, and so the children of Israel when they came out of Egypt. And even today when they take up their pens and date 1876 years—when do they date from? Why, from the blood of Christ. Everything dates from blood. In this chapter we see the command to sacrifice. They slew the lamb. God didn't say, "Put a lamb to your front door, and I will spare you," but on the houses.

Some groups of people say, "Preach anything but the death; preach the life of Christ." You may preach that, and you'll never save a soul. It is not Christ's sympathy— His life—we preach, it is His sacrifice. That's what brings men out of darkness. I can imagine some proud Egyptians that day, who when they heard the bleating of the lambs—there must have been over two hundred thousand lambs—saying, "What an absurd performance. Every man has got a lamb, and they have got the best lambs out of the flock, too, and they are going to cover their houses with the blood." They looked upon this as an absurd proceeding—a flaw in their character. You may find a good many flaws in your character, but you cannot find a flaw in the Lamb of God.

When the hour came, you could see them all slaying their lambs, and not only that, but putting the blood on the doorposts. To those Egyptians or to the men of the world, how absurd it looked. They probably said, "Why are you disfiguring your houses in that way?" It was not upon the threshold. God didn't want that, but they were to put it upon the lintels and doorposts—where God could see it that night so that (thirteenth verse) He might see it as a token. This blood was to be a substitution for death, and all who hadn't that token in the land of Egypt had their first-born smitten at midnight. There was a wail from Egypt from one end to the other. But death didn't come near the homes where there was the token. It was death that kept death out of the dwelling.

Many people say, "I wish I was as good as that woman who has been ministering to the sick for the last fifty years. I would feel sure of heaven." My friends, if you have the blood behind you, you are as safe as anybody on this earth. It is not because that woman has been living a life of sacrifices in her ministrations to the poor that she will enter the kingdom of God. It is not our life of good deeds or our righteousness that will take us to heaven, but the atonement. And the question ought to come to everyone tonight, "Are we sheltered behind the blood?" If not, death will come by-and-by and you will be separated from God for eternity. If you have not a substitute you will die. Death is passed upon all of us. Why? Because of our sin. If we have not a substitute we have no hope.

Not only were they to have a token, but they were to do something else. We read in the eleventh verse, "And thus shall ye eat it; with your loins girded, your shoes on your feet, and your staff in your hand; and ye shall eat it in haste; it is the Lord's passover." Now a great many people wonder why they haven't got more spiritual power and have not the joy of the Lord with them all the time. It is because they haven't got the blood of the lamb with them. These pilgrims had a long journey before them, and the Lord told them to eat the lamb. If we feed upon the Lamb we will get strength in proportion. My friends, be sure before you commence on your pilgrimage that you are sheltered behind the blood, for when He sees the blood, death will pass over you. And let me ask this assemblage tonight if every one of you have the token.

I was speaking to a man some time ago, who, when I asked him if he had the token said, "I have a prayer," and when he got to heaven he would pray, and he thought that would admit him. I said to him, "You won't get in that way. You must be cleansed by the blood of Christ. That is the only power that will open the gates of heaven—the only countersign."

When I went east the other night, the conductor came around and called for the tickets. I pulled out my ticket and he punched it. He didn't know whether it was a white or a black man who presented it, I believe. He didn't care who it was; all he wanted was the token. So all that God wants is the token of our salvation. It doesn't depend upon our deeds, our righteousness, or upon our lives; it depends upon whether or not we are sheltered behind the blood. That is the question. It didn't matter in that land of Goshen whether the child was six months or years old if it was behind the blood. It was not their moral character, nor their connections, but the blood that saved them. It is the atonement that saves, and that is the teaching all through your Bible.

There is another verse in the twenty-ninth chapter of Exodus I want to call your attention to: "And thou shalt slay the ram, and thou shalt take his blood, and sprinkle it round about upon the altar." Now we see that Aaron the high priest could not come to God with his prayers alone. He had to sprinkle the blood upon the altar. There was a time when I didn't believe in the substitution and in the blood, and my prayers went no higher than my head; but when I came to God by Jesus Christ—by the way of blood—it was different. I never knew a man who came to God really but who came this way. That great high priest had to come this way, too.

Then, again in the thirtieth chapter, tenth verse, we see, "And Aaron shall make an atonement upon the horns of it once in a year with the blood of the sin offering of atonements: once in the year shall he make atonement upon it throughout your generations: it is most holy unto the LORD." Now, an atonement is the only thing that makes a sinner and God one—is the only thing that will bring God and the sinner together. I would like, if I had time, to give you all the passages touching upon atonement in the Old Testament, but it would take too long.

Turn again to the eighth chapter of Leviticus. This book of Leviticus is one of the most valuable, because it relates all about the worship of God. I remember when I used to read this book I used to wonder what it was all about—a verse like this, for instance: "And he slew it; and Moses took of the blood of it, and put it upon the tip of Aaron's right ear, and upon the thumb of his right hand, and upon the great toe of his right foot." I would say, "What does this mean? 'Put it upon the tip of Aaron's right ear.'" What for? I think I have got a little light upon the subject since those days. "Blood upon the ear?" So that a man could hear the voice of God, of course. And so a man who has accepted the atonement can hear the Word rightly. Blood upon the hand of a man, so that he who works for God can work rightly. Hundreds of men think they are working out their salvation, and they are only deceiving themselves. Bear in mind then that a man cannot do anything until he is sheltered behind the blood. When a man is in this position then he can go and be acceptable to God. Then blood upon the feet, so that a man can walk with God. You know when God came to Adam he hid himself. He hadn't the blood, and he couldn't walk with God. He put those people in question behind the blood, and He walked among them. When they came to the Red Sea the mighty waters opened, and God walked with them. In the wilderness they wanted water, and a rod struck the rock, and a crystal stream gushed forth. Why? Because they had had the substitution.

Many people say this is a very mysterious thing. We

don't understand why God wants blood as an atonement. A man said to me, "I detest your religion; I hate your God." "Why?" I asked. "I detest a God who demands blood," he replied. Now, God is not an unjust God. He doesn't demand it without giving us a reason. He tells us in His Word that "the life of the flesh is in the blood." Take the blood out of me and I am a dead man. Life has been forfeited, the law has been broken, and the penalty must come upon us, and His blood He gives us is life; it is the life of our flesh. Three times we see "blood" mentioned in the twenty-third and twenty-fourth verses, and the reason is that it is life. You and I have lost life by the Fall, and what we want is to get back that life we lost, and we have it offered to us by the atonement of Christ. I have often thought I would far rather be out of Eden and have the blood than be in Eden without it. Adam might have been there ten years, and Satan might have been there ten years, and Satan might have come and got him. But some can't see why God permitted Adam to fall. They can't begin to discern the philosophy of it. They can't see why God ever permitted original sin to come into the world. The best answer to that was given by the Reverend Andrew Bonair, who said, "It was a great deal more wonderful that God should send His Son down to bear the brunt of it." Let us thank God we have a refuge, a substitute for the sin we are groaning under.

Turn to the fifty-third chapter of Isaiah. You hear a good many people saying, "I don't believe in the Old Testament, I believe in the New." My friends, both are inseparable. A scarlet thread runs through the two and binds them together. "We, like sheep, have gone astray," but "he was wounded for our transgressions, he was bruised for our iniquities: the chastisement of our peace was upon him; and with his stripes we are healed." My friends, in the fifty-third chapter of Isaiah we see it prophesied seven hundred years before it took place that He would die and be a substitute for you and me, that we might live. And now, my friends, let us accept Him. It seems base ingratitude not to praise God every hour of our lives that He has given such a Savior. Let us take time. Many a young man thinks it noble to scoff at this; I think it the basest ingratitude. This atonement is the only hope of my eternal life. Take the doctrine of substitution out of my Bible, and I would not take it home with me tonight. Let us praise God that He loved us so as to give us His only Son so that we might be saved.

I remember some years ago reading about a New York family. A young man, during the gold fever, went out to the Pacific, and left his wife and little boy. Just as soon as he was successful he was going to send money. A long time elapsed, but at last a letter came enclosing a draft, and telling his wife to come on. The woman took a passage in one of the fine steamers of the Pacific line, full of hope and joy at the prospect of soon being united to her husband. They had not been out many days when a voice went ringing through the ship, "Fire! Fire!" The pumps were set to work and the buckets were brought into operation, but the fire gained upon them. There was a powder magazine on board, and the captain ordered all the boats to be instantly lowered. He knew whenever the fire reached the powder they would all be lost. The people scrambled into the boats and the mother and boy were left on deck. As the last boat was being pushed off the woman begged to be taken in. The majority insisted the boat was too full, and wanted to push off, but one man put in a word for her, and they said they could allow one more on board, but no more. What did the mother do? Did she go on board and leave her son? No. She put her boy into that lifeboat and told him if he ever lived to see his father to tell him, "I died to save you." And the boat pulled away from that ship, and left the mother standing there. The vessel went on burning. Presently an explosion was heard, and all was buried in the ocean. Suppose that young man was here tonight. Suppose you spoke to him about the act of his mother, and he turned round and scoffed at it. "Why," you would say, "that ungrateful wretch doesn't deserve to live," and this is what you are doing. He laid down His life for you. Now will you speak contemptuously about Him? Will you speak lightly of the blood laid down on Calvary for you? Let us rather all thank God we have such a Savior. Let us live for Him when He died for us.

Part Two

You who were here last night remember that we spoke of the precious blood, and that we looked at a few passages in the Old Testament bearing upon the subject. Tonight I want to take up some passages referring to the subject in the New Testament. Soon after we came back from Europe to this country, I received a letter from a lady saying that she had looked forward to our coming back to this country with a great deal of interest, and that her interest remained after we had commenced our services until I came to the lecture on the blood when she gave up all hope of our doing any good. In closing that letter, she said, "Where did Jesus ever teach the perilous and barbarous doctrine that men were to be redeemed by the shedding of His blood? Never, never did Jesus teach that monstrous idea."

Let us turn to the fourteenth chapter of Mark, twenty-fourth verse, and we will find, "And he said unto them, This is my blood of the new testament, which is shed for many," and also in Matthew, twenty-sixth chapter and twenty-eighth verse: "For this is my blood of the new testament, which is shed for many for the remission of sins." There are a good many passages, but it is not necessary to refer to more. If Christ did not teach it, and also the apostles—if Christ did not preach it, then I have read my Bible wrong all these years. I haven't got the key to the Scriptures; it is a sealed book to me, and if I don't preach it—if I give it up, I've nothing left to preach. Take the blessed doctrine of the blood out of my Bible, and my capital is gone, and I've got to take to something else.

I remember when in the old country, a young man came to me—a minister came round to me and said he wanted to talk with me. He said to me, "Mr. Moody, you are either all right, and I am all wrong, or else I am right, and you are all wrong." "Well, sir," said I, "you have the advantage of me. You have heard me preach, and know what doctrines I hold, whereas, I have not heard you, and don't know what you preach." "Well," said he, "the difference between your preaching and mine is that you make out that salvation is got by Christ's death, and I make out that it is attained by His life." "Now, what do you do with the passages bearing upon the death?" And I quoted the passages, "Without the shedding of blood there is no remission," and "He Himself, bore our own sins by His own body on the tree," and asked him what he did with them, for instance. "I never preach on them at all." I quoted a number of passages more, and he gave me the same answer. "Well, what do you preach?" I finally asked. "Moral essays," he replied. Said I, "Did you ever know anybody to be saved by that kind of thing— did you ever convert anybody by them?" "I never aimed at that kind of conversion; I mean to get men to heaven by culture—by refinement." "Well," said I, "if I didn't preach those texts, and only preached culture, the whole thing would be a sham." "And it is a sham to me," was his reply. I tell you the moment a man breaks away from this doctrine of blood, religion becomes a sham, because the whole teaching of this book is of one story, and this is that Christ came into the world, and died for our sins.

I want to call your attention to the nineteenth chapter of John, and the thirty-fourth verse: "But one of the soldiers with a spear pierced his side, and forthwith came there out blood and water." There came out blood and water. Now, it was prophesied years before, that there should open a fountain, which should wash away sin and uncleanness, and it seems that this fountain was opened here by the spear of the soldier, and out of the fountain came blood and water. It was the breaking of the crown of hell, and the giving of the crown to heaven. When the Roman soldier drove out the blood, out came the water, and it touched that spear, and it was not long before Christ had that Roman government. It is a throne and a footstool now, and by-and-by it will sway the earth from pole to pole. This earth has been redeemed by the blessed blood of Christ. Peter says in his first Epistle, first chapter, eighteenth and nineteenth verses:

> Forasmuch as ye know that ye were not redeemed with corruptible things, as silver and gold, from your vain conversation received by tradition from your fathers; But with the precious blood of Christ, as of a lamb without blemish and without spot.

You are not redeemed by such corruptible things as gold or silver, but by the precious blood of the Lamb—"the precious blood of Christ—as of a lamb without blemish."

If silver and gold could have redeemed us, it would have been the easiest thing to have made a pile of gold ten thousand times larger than the bulk of the earth. But gold couldn't do it. Why, the poorest thing in heaven is gold. As I said last night, the law had been broken, and the penalty of death had come upon us, and it required life to redeem us. Now, it says we shall be redeemed. My friends, redemption is to me one of the most precious treasures in the Word of God—to think that Christ has bought me by his blood. I am no longer my own, I am His. He has ransomed me.

A friend of mine once told me that he was going out from Dublin one day, and met a boy who had one of those

English sparrows in his hand. It was frightened and just seemed to sit as if it pined for liberty, but the boy held it so tight that it could not get away. The boy's strength was too much for the bird. My friend said, "Open your hand and let the bird go. You will never tame him; he is wild." But the boy replied, "Faith an' I'll not; I've been a whole hour trying to catch him, an' now I've got him, I'm going to keep him." So the man took out his purse and asked the boy if he would sell it. A bargain was made, and the sparrow was transferred to the man's hand. He opened his hand, and at first it did not seem to realize it had liberty, but by-and-by it flew away, and as it went it chirped, as much as to say, "You have redeemed me." And so Christ has come down and offered to redeem us and give us liberty when we were bound with sin. Satan was stronger than we were. He has had six thousand years' experience. He did not come to buy us from Satan, but from the penalty of our sin.

Another thought about the blood. It makes us all one. The blood brings us into one family, into the household of faith. I remember during the war Dr. Kirk, one of the most eloquent men I ever heard, was speaking in Boston. At that time, you recollect, there was a good deal said about the Irish and the black man, and what an amount of talk about the war of races. He said while preaching one night, "I saw a poor Irishman and a black man and an Englishman, and the blood of Christ came down and fell upon them and made them one." My friends, it brings nationalities together, it brings those scattered with the seeds of discord together and makes them one. Let us turn to Acts seventeen, verse twenty-six, and we read, "And hath made of one blood all nations of men for to dwell on all the face of the earth, and hath determined the times before appointed, and the bounds of their habitation." That's what the blood of Christ does. It just makes us one. I can tell [men] that [have] been redeemed by the blood. They speak all the same language. I don't require to be in [their] company ten minutes before I can tell whether or not [they have] been redeemed. They have only one language, and you can tell when they speak whether they are outside the blood or sheltered by it. The blood has two voices—one is for salvation and the other is for condemnation. The blood tonight cries out for my salvation or for my condemnation. If we are sheltered behind the blood, it cries for our salvation, for we see in Galatians, "It cries for our peace." There is no peace till a man has been sheltered by that blood.

Again, I would like to call your attention to the twenty-sixth chapter of Matthew, twenty-eighth verse, where we find Christ speaking of His blood: "For this is my blood of the new testament, which is shed for . . . the remission of sins." This blood was "shed for the remission of sins." Then in Hebrews ninth chapter and twenty-second verse, where it says, "without shedding of blood is no remission [of sins]." Men don't realize that this is God's plan of salvation. Said a man to me last night after the meeting, "Why, God has got a plan to save us." Certainly He has. You must be saved by God's plan. It was love that prompted God to send His Son to save us and shed His blood. That was the plan. And without the blood what hope have you? There is not a sin from your childhood—from your cradle—up till now that can be forgiven, unless by the blood. Let us take God at his word: "Without the shedding of blood there is no remission [of sins]." Without the blood, [there is] no remission whatever. I don't see how a man can fail to comprehend this. That's what Christ died for; that's what Christ died on Calvary for. If a man makes light of that blood what hope has he? How are you going to get into the kingdom of God? You cannot join in the song of the saints if you don't go into heaven that way. You cannot sing the song of redemption. If you did I suppose you would be off in some corner with a harp of your own and singing, "I saved myself; I saved myself." You can't get in that way.

You must accept the plan of redemption and come in through it. "He that climbeth up some other way, the same is a thief and a robber."

Then, in the tenth chapter of Hebrews, we find Paul, if he wrote this, just taking up the very thought, "He that despised Moses' law died without mercy under two or three witnesses." You know when a man made light of the Law under the Mosaic dispensation, whenever two witnesses came into court and swore that he hadn't kept the Law, they just took him out and stoned him to death. Take up the next verse: "Of how much surer punishment suppose ye shall be thought worthy who hath trodden under foot the Son of God and hath counted the blood of the covenant wherewith He was sanctified an unholy thing, and hath done despite unto the spirit of grace."

My friends, what hope is there if a man tramples the blood of Christ under his foot, if he says, "I will have nothing to do with that blood"? I ask in all candor, what mercy is there? What hope has he if he "hath trodden underfoot the Son of God and hath counted the blood of the covenant wherewith He was sanctified an unholy thing"? This is the only way to get to heaven—no other way. Turn again to the twelfth verse of the same chapter and we see, "But this man, after he had offered one sacrifice for sins"—mark that, He had settled the question of sin—"forever, sat down on the right hand of God."

The high priests could never sit down. Their work was never done; but our High Priest hath put sin away by one sacrifice and then ascended to God. And in this same chapter of Hebrews we see again, "Having therefore, brethren, boldness to enter into the holiest by the blood of Jesus, by a new and living way, which He hath consecrated for us through the vail, that is to say, his flesh, and having an High Priest over the house of God, let us draw near with a true heart, in full assurance of faith, having our hearts sprinkled from an evil conscience, and our bodies washed with pure water. Let us hold fast the profession of our faith without wavering, for He is faithful that promised." I want to call your attention to the twentieth verse more particularly—"By a new and living way." Now Christ has opened a new and living way. We cannot get to heaven by our own deeds now. He has opened "a new and a living way."

We don't need a high priest to go once a year and pray to God. Thank God we are all kings and all priests. We can go straight to the Father in the name of the Lord Jesus Christ. When Christ died the temple veil was rent from the top to the bottom—not from the bottom to the top—and every poor son of Adam can walk right in and worship—right into the presence of God, if he only comes by the way of the blood. Yes, thank God, He has opened a new and a living way whereby we can come to Him. Let us thank God for the new and the living way. We don't need any bishop, we don't need any pope, we don't need any priest or prophet now; but everyone can be made king and priest, and we can come through this living way to His presence and ask Him to take away our sins. There's not a man in this assembly but can come to Him tonight.

There's a good deal about the blood in Hebrews that I would like to bring up; time passes, and I have just to fly through the subject. Now I don't know any doctrine I have preached that has been talked about more than the doctrine of blood. Why, the moment Satan gets a man to leave out this doctrine of blood, he has gained all he wants. It is the most pernicious idea to leave it out. A man may be a brilliant preacher, may have a brilliant intellect, and he may have large crowds of people, but if he leaves this out, no one will be blessed under his ministry, no one will be born into God's kingdom. If a man leaves out this blood he may as well go and whistle in the streets and try to convert people that way, for all the good he will do in saving souls.

It is said that old Dr. Alexander of Princeton College,

when a young student used to start out to preach, always gave him a piece of advice. The old man would stand with his gray locks and his venerable face and say, "Young man, make much of the blood in your ministry." Now, I have traveled considerably during the past few years, and never met a minister who made much of the blood and much of the atonement but God had blessed his ministry, and souls were born into the light by it. But a man who leaves it out, the moment he goes, his church falls to pieces like a rope of sand, and his preaching has been barren of good result.

And so if you find a man preaching who has covered up this doctrine of blood, don't sit under his ministry; I don't care what denomination he belongs to, get out of it. Fly from it as those who flew from Sodom. Never mind how you get out of it—leave it. It is a whitened sepulcher. There is no life if they don't preach the blood. It is the only way we've got to conquer Satan, the only way we can enter heaven, and we cannot get there unless we have washed our robes in the blood of the Lamb. If we expect to conquer we must be first washed by that blood. A man who has not realized what the blood has done for him has not the token of salvation.

It is told of Julian the apostate, that while he was fighting he received an arrow in his side. He pulled it out, and taking a handful of blood threw it into the air, and cried, "Galilean, Galilean, thou hast conquered!" Yes, the Galilean is going to conquer, and you must bear in mind if you don't accept the blood—don't submit to it and let it cleanse you—the rocks will fall on you, because the decree of heaven is that every knee will bow to the will of heaven. The blood is a call of mercy now. He wants you to come—He beseeches you to accept and be saved.

I heard of an old minister who had preached the gospel for fifty years faithfully. "Ah!" many here will say, "I wish I was as safe to go to heaven as he." When he was reaching his end he asked that his Bible should be brought to him. His eyes were growing dim in death, and he said to one of those about him, "I wish you would turn to the first epistle of John, chapter one, verse seven," and when it was found, the old man put his dying finger on the passage where it says, "But if we walk in the light as he is in light, we have fellowship one with another, and the blood of Jesus Christ his Son cleanseth us from all sin." And he said, "I die in the hope of that." It was the blood in his ministry that cleansed him. And so it is the only way by which our sins can be washed away. Why, there was a question once asked in heaven when a great crowd were gathering there, "Who are those?" And the answer was, "They are those who have come by great tribulation and have been washed by the blood of the Lamb."

Now, the question here tonight is, what are you going to do with that blood? We have had it for two nights, and before I close I would like to ask you, what are you going to do about it? You must do either of two things—take it or reject it. Trample it underfoot or cleanse your sins by it. I heard of a lady who told a servant to cook a lamb. She told him how to do it up and all about it, but she didn't tell him what to do with the blood. So he went to her and asked, "What are you going to do with the blood of the lamb?" She had been under conviction for some time, and such a question went like an arrow to her soul. She went to her room and felt uneasy, and the question kept continually coming to her, "What are you going to do with the blood of the lamb," and before morning she was on her knees asking for the mercy of the blood of the Lamb.

Now the most solemn truth in the gospel is that the only thing He left down here is His blood. His body and bones He took away, but He left His blood on Calvary. There is either of two things we must do. One is to send back the message to heaven that we don't want the blood of Christ to cleanse us of our sin, or else accept it. Why, when we come to our dying hour the blood will be worth more than all the kingdoms of the world to us. Can you afford to turn your back upon it and make light of it?

Dr. King, when the war was going on, went down to the field with the Christian Commission. He used to go among the soldiers, and during one of his visits he heard a man cry, "Blood! Blood! Blood!" He thought that, as the man had just been taken off the battlefield, the scene of carnage and blood was still upon his mind. The doctor went to him, and tried to talk to the man about Christ, and to divert his mind from the scenes of the field. "Ah, Doctor," said the man, feebly, "I was not thinking of the battlefield, but of the blood of Christ"; and he whispered the word "blood" once more and was gone.

Dear friends, do you want all your sins washed away from you? [The blood] was shed for the remission of sins, and without the shedding of blood there would be no remission. There is blood on the mercy seat tonight. "I am not looking to your sins now," God says, "but come and press in, press in, and receive remission." Thank God, the blood is still on the mercy seat. It is there, and He beseeches you to accept it. What more can He do for your salvation? Now, my friends, don't go out of this tabernacle laughing and scoffing at the precious offering made to you, but just bow your head now and lift up your voice, "O God of heaven, may the blood of Thy Son cleanse me from all sin." The blood is sufficient.

Some years ago I was journeying to the Pacific coast, and nearly every stagedriver I met was talking about a prominent stagedriver who had just died. You know that in driving over these rocky roads they depend a good deal upon the brake. This poor man, when he was dying, was heard to say, "I am on the down grade and cannot keep the brake." Just about that time one of the most faithful men of God, Alfred Cookman, passed away. His wife and friends gathered around his deathbed, and when his last moments arrived, it seemed as if heaven had opened before him, as with a shout he cried, "I am sweeping through the gates washed by the blood of the Lamb." What a comfort this must have been to his friends. What a comfort it must have been to him, the blood of the atonement in his last hours.

My friends, if you want a glorious end like the end of that sainted man you must come to the blood of Christ.

Moody sought to address the many excuses used by individuals to avoid any commitment to Christ.

One of the more popular excuses focused on the integrity of the Bible. Moody recognized the fact that belief in the Bible was paramount. To him, the problem was not the book but those who attacked it—for, in his mind, they never read the Bible carefully.

Other excuses abounded: God is a hard master; Christianity makes one gloomy; if I'm one of the elect I'll make it no matter what; too many hypocrites in the Church; I have plenty of time; I am too bad; I cannot believe. Moody stipulated that no excuse was adequate. No excuse could ever prevail over the need to come to Christ.

CHAPTER SIX

Excuses

Part One

Mr. Moody then said the text he would take was to be found in [Luke chapter fourteen] the nineteenth verse: "I pray thee have me excused." Christ had been invited to dine with a rich Pharisee, and it seemed as though this man had gathered his friends together in a kind of conspiracy to catch Christ. They watched Him. A man who had dropsy was placed before Jesus, as though they wanted to see what He would do. Christ read their hearts, and so before them He healed the man. He asked them if it was lawful to heal on the Sabbath day. But they didn't want to answer for fear they'd betray themselves, and so they held their peace. Then Christ put the question to them in another way and asked them if any of them had an ox or an ass fall into the pit, should he not straightway pull it out on the Sabbath day? And then He healed the man, as the Pharisees and lawyers weren't able to answer Him.

Then He told them about the feast, and told them to be

humble. When a man prepares a feast, men rush in, but when God prepares one they all begin to make excuses, and don't want to go. The first excuse was that made by Adam, "The woman Thou gavest me, she gave me to eat." These men that excused themselves made manufactured excuses; they didn't really have any. The drunkard, the libertine, the businessman, the citizen, the harlot, all had their excuses. If God were to take men at their word about these excuses, and swept every one into his grave who had an excuse, there would be a very small congregation in the tabernacle next Sunday; there would be little business in Chicago, and in a few weeks the grass would be growing on these busy streets. Every man who was nursing a sin had an excuse, as though God had asked them to go into a plague-stricken city, or a hospital, or to hear a dry lecture, or something repelling and objectionable, something that wasn't for their greatest good.

Take the excuses. There wasn't one that wasn't a lie. The devil made them all; and if the sinner hadn't one already, the devil was there at his elbow to suggest one about the truth of the Bible, or something of that sort. One of the excuses mentioned was that the man invited had bought a piece of ground, and had to look at it. Real estate and corner lots were keeping a good many men out of God's kingdom. It was a lie to say that he had to go and see it then, for he ought to have looked at it before he bought it. Then the next man said he'd bought some oxen and must prove them. That was another lie; for if he hadn't proved them before he bought them as he ought to have done, he could have done it after the supper just as well as before it. But the third man had the silliest, the worst, excuse of all; he said he had married a wife, and couldn't come. Why didn't he bring her with him? She'd have liked the supper just as well as he would and would have enjoyed a supper, as almost any young bride would.

These seemed to be foolish excuses, but they were not

any more so than the excuses of today. Indeed, the excuses of men are getting worse and worse all the time. They say they can't believe the Bible; it's so mysterious. Well, what of it? Infidels, skeptics, pantheists, deists, said they didn't believe the Bible. Had they ever used it? Did they read it as carefully as they read any other book? This was their excuse. If everybody could understand everything the Bible said it wouldn't be God's Book. If Christians, if theologians had studied it for forty, fifty, sixty years, and only then began to understand it, how could a man expect to understand it by one reading? A child the first day at school couldn't even know the alphabet, and yet it wasn't a sign that it was a poor school because he didn't learn the first day all about grammar, arithmetic, and geometry. Another said God was a hard master. No; that was one of Satan's lies. The devil's the hard master. In the Tombs in New York there is over the door the remark, "The way of the transgressor is hard." God's yoke is easy, His burden light. Ask prisoners, ask gamblers, ask sinners, if Satan's yoke is easy. It's the hardest of all . . . Is God a hard master, Christians? . . . God's service a hard one? How will that sound in the Judgment? Many said it wasn't that, but there is such a struggle. Wasn't all life a struggle? Some said they were wicked. Those are just the kind Jesus came to save. They weren't too wicked to be saved. They were so worldly minded, so hard-hearted; that was another falsehood.

Look at what God did for Bunyan and John Newton, and many others who were the [most] wicked, and even the thief on the cross. God is already reconciled; He doesn't need the sinner to be reconciled to Him. The Lord prepares the sinner.

A touching story was told of an English father and son, who had become estranged, but who were united over the deathbed of the wife and mother. The father was stern, but he was reconciled by the prayers of the dying parent. And this was so with God: the sinner had left Him, God was removed from him, but God and the sinner were brought near by the death of our Lord Jesus Christ.

This afternoon I chose for my text the fourteenth verse of the fourteenth chapter of Luke, and you will remember I took up certain of the excuses of the present day in regard to accepting Christ. One of these excuses I said was that Christ was a hard master; it was a very difficult thing to become a Christian, and the other was that Christ would not receive them. Now, I just want to take up where I left off, and notice the excuses we hear in the inquiry room, in the streets of Chicago—everywhere. I said this afternoon you were not invited, when asked to come to Christ, to a dry lecture on a disagreeable subject but to a marriage feast. The Lord has said, "Blessed is he who shall be at the marriage supper of the Lord." I have missed a good many appointments in my life, but there is one I will not miss. I would rather be at the marriage feast than have the whole world rolled at my feet. I want to be there and sit down with Isaac and Jacob and Abraham at that supper. It is an invitation for joy and gladness that comes from the King of Kings, from the Lord of Glory, to every man and woman in this assembly—the invitation to be at the marriage supper of the Lamb. It is not a personal invitation, but a universal one—"Go out into the highways and hedges and compel them to come in, that my house may be filled." Bid them come, "the poor and the maimed and the halt and the blind," to the marriage feast, prepared at great expense by our blessed Redeemer. I said in the afternoon that people began to make excuses very early in the history of Christianity, and they are still at it. Nineteen hundred years have rolled away and still there are excuses. One of the excuses that we very often hear people giving is that they don't want to become Christians because it will make them gloomy—they will have to put on long faces, button their coats up, cut off all joy, and walk through the world till they get to heaven, where they will have pleasure forevermore. We look forward to that happy future, but thank God, we have some pleasure here. Indeed, no man in the world should be so happy as a man of God. It is one continual source of gladness. He can look up and say, "God is my Father," "Christ is my Savior, and the church is my mother." All who think otherwise than that a Christian's life is one of unceasing joy are deceiving themselves.

I was going by a saloon the other day and saw a sign, "Drink and be merry." Poor, blind, deluded fellows, if they think this will make them merry. If you want to be merry you must come to the living fountain that bursts from the throne of God; then you will have true pleasure. A man away from God cannot have true pleasure. He is continually thirsting for something he cannot get—thirsting for something that can quench his thirst, and he cannot get it until he comes to the living fountain. My friends, that is just another wile of the devil to keep men from grace. It is false. The more a man is lifted up to heaven the more joy and peace and gladness he has. He is lifted away from gloom.

Look at a man on his way to execution. Suppose I run up to him, holding out my hand, and say, "There is a pardon that has been signed by the Governor," and I give it him. Would he be gloomy and joyless? That is Christ. He comes down with a pardon to us poor men and women on our way to execution. Yonder is a man starving. I go to him and give him bread. Is that going to make him gloomy? A poor man comes along crying with thirst, and I give him a glass of ice water; would that make him gloomy? That is what Christ is doing for us. He has a well of living water, and He asks every thirsty soul to drink freely. Don't you believe for a moment that Christianity is going to make you gloomy.

I remember when I was a boy I thought I would wait

till I [was about to] die and then become a Christian. I thought if I had consumption, or some lingering disease, I would have plenty of time to become one, and in the meantime, I would enjoy the best of the pleasures of the world. My friends, I was at that time under the power of the devil. The idea that a man has more pleasure away from church is one of the devil's lies. Do not believe it, but accept of this universal invitation to the marriage feast.

Part Two

I can imagine some men saying, "Mr. Moody has not touched my case at all. That is not the reason why I won't accept Christ. I don't know if I am one of the elect." How often am I met with this excuse—how often do I hear it in the inquiry room! How many men fold their arms and say, "If I am one of the elect I will be saved, and if I am not I won't. No use in your bothering about it." Why don't some of those [businessmen] say, "If God is going to make me a successful [businessman] in Chicago I will be one whether I like it or not, and if he hasn't I won't."

If you are sick and a doctor prescribes for you, don't take the medicine; throw it out of the door; it doesn't matter, for if God has decreed you are going to die you will, and if He hasn't you will get better. If you use that argument you may as well not walk home from this tabernacle. If God has said you'll get home, you'll get [there]—you'll fly through the air if you have been elected to go home. These illustrations are just the same as the excuse. You cannot go up there and give that excuse. The water of life is offered freely to everyone.

No unconverted man in the wide, wide world has anything to do with the doctrine of election any more than I have to do with the government of China. The epistle of Paul was written to godly men. Suppose I pick up a letter and open it, and it tells me about the death of my wife. Dear me—my wife, dead. But I look on the other side of the letter and find that it is directed to another man. And so a great many people take Paul's letter to the churches and take it as a personal letter. This is what you have to take up: "Whosoever will, let him drink of the water of life freely." He came down sixty years after His resurrection and said to John—put it so broadly that no one will mistake it; put it so broadly that no one in Chicago can be stumbling over it, so that all men may see it plainly—"Whosoever will, let him drink of the water of life freely." If you will, you will; if you won't, you won't.

Do you think that God will come down here to give you salvation, without giving you the power to take it, and then condemn you to eternity for not taking it? With the gift comes the power, and you can take it and live if you will. Don't stumble over election anymore. You have to deal with that broad proclamation: "Whosoever will, let him drink of the waters of life freely."

I can imagine someone in the gallery clear up there saying, "I never have bothered my head about election, I don't believe men are gloomy when they become Christians. If I was alone I would tell you my reason, but I do not like to get up in this large assembly and talk here. The fact is there are hypocrites in the churches. I know a man, a prominent man in the church, who cheated me out of twenty-five dollars. I won't accept this invitation because of those hypocrites in the churches." My friend, you will find very few there if you get to heaven. There won't be a hypocrite in the next world, and if you don't want to be associated with hypocrites in the next world, you will take this invitation. Why, you will find hypocrites everywhere. One of the apostles was himself the very prince of hypocrites, but he didn't get to heaven. You will find plenty of hypocrites in the church. They have been there for the last eighteen hundred years and will probably remain there. But what is that to you? This is an individual matter between you and your God. Is it because there are hypocrites that you are not going to accept the invitation?

"Ah, well, Mr. Moody, that is not my case. I am a businessman, and I have no time. Since the Chicago fire I have had as much as I could attend to in recovering what I lost." I believe if I stood at the door and asked anyone who went out to accept the invitation, I believe hundreds of you would say, "Mr. Moody, you will have to excuse me tonight; time is very precious with me, and you'll have to excuse me." What have you been doing the last twenty, thirty, forty, fifty years that you haven't had a moment to devote to the acceptance of the invitation? That is the cry of the world today: "Time is precious; business must be attended to, and we have no time to spare." Some of you will say, "I cannot wait; I have to go home and put the children to bed; this is more important." My friends, to accept this invitation is more important than anything else in the world. There is nothing in the world that is so important as the question of accepting the invitation. How many mechanics in this building have spent five years learning their trade, in order to support their families and support themselves a few years—forty or fifty years at the longest? How many professional men have toiled and worked hard for years to get such an education that they might go out to the world and cope with it, and during all these years have not had a minute to seek their salvation? Is that a legitimate excuse? Tell Him tonight that you haven't time or let this be the night—the hour—cost you what it will, when you shall say, "By the grace of God, I will accept the invitation and press up to the marriage supper of the Lamb."

"Oh, but that is not my case," says another, "I have time. If I thought I could become a Christian I would sit here all night and let business and everything else go, and I would press into the kingdom of God. I am not fit to become a Christian, that's the trouble with me." He says, "Go into the highways and hedges," and "bring in hither the poor, and the maimed, and the halt and the blind,"—just invite them all, without distinction of sect or creed, station or nationality; never mind whether they are rich or poor. If the Lord doesn't complain about your fitness, you shouldn't look to see if you have the right kind of clothes.

I had to notice during the war, when enlisting was going on, sometimes a man would come up with a nice silk hat on, patent leather boots, nice kid gloves, and a fine suit of clothes, which probably cost him one hundred dollars; perhaps the next man who came along would be a hodcarrier, dressed in the poorest kind of clothes. Both had to strip alike and put on the regimental uniform. So when you come and say you are not fit, haven't got good clothes, haven't got righteousness enough, remember that He will furnish you with the uniform of heaven, and you will be set down at the marriage feast of the Lamb.

I don't care how black and vile your heart may be, only accept the invitation of Jesus Christ, and He will make you fit to sit down with the rest at that feast. How many are continually crying out, "I am too bad; no use [in my] trying to become a Christian." This is the way the devil works. Sometimes he will say to a man, "You don't want to be saved; you're good enough already," and he will point to some black-hearted hypocrite and say, "Look at him and see how you appear in comparison; you are far better than he is." But by-and-by the man gets a glimpse of the blackness of his own heart, and his conscience troubles him. Then says the devil, "You are too bad to be saved; the Lord won't save such as you; you are too vile; you must get better before you try to get God to save you." And so men try to make themselves better and instead get worse all the time. The gospel bids you come as you are. Seek first the kingdom of heaven—make no delay; come just as you are.

I heard of an artist who wanted to get a man to sit for a

painting of the prodigal son. He went down to the alms-houses and the prisons but couldn't get one. Going through the streets one day he found a poor wretched man, a beggar, coming along, and he asked him if he would sit for the study. He said he would. A bargain was made, and the artist gave him his address. The time for the appointment arrived, and the beggar duly appeared and said to the artist, "I have come to keep that appointment which I made with you." "An appointment with me?" replied the artist; "You are mistaken; I have an appointment with a beggar today." "Well," said the man, "I am that beggar, but I thought I would put on a new suit of clothes before I came to see you." "I don't want you," was the artist's reply, "I want a beggar." And so a great many people come to God with their self-righteousness, instead of coming in their raggedness. Why, someone has said, "It is only the ragged sinners that open God's wardrobe. If you want to start out to get a pair of shoes from a passer-by, you would start out barefooted, wouldn't you?"

I remember a boy to whom I gave a pair of boots, and I found him shortly after in his bare feet again. I asked him what he had done with them, and he replied that when he was dressed up it spoiled his business. When he was dressed up no one would give him anything. By keeping his feet naked he got as many as five pairs of boots a day. So if you want to come to God, don't dress yourself up. It is the naked sinners God wants to save. Come to Him after you have cast off your self-righteousness, and the Son of God will receive you.

I remember some years ago a man who had gone to sea. He led a wild, reckless life. When his mother was alive she was a praying mother. (Ah, how many men have been saved by their mothers after they have gone up to heaven.) And perhaps her influence made him think sometimes. When at sea a desire [to] lead a better life came over him, and when he got on shore he thought he would join the Free Masons. He made application, but, upon investigation, his character proved he was only a drunken sailor, and he was blackballed. He next thought of joining the Odd Fellows, and applied, but his application met with a like result. While he was walking up Fulton Street one day a little tract was given him—an invitation to the prayer meeting. He came, and Christ received him. I remember him getting up in the meeting, and telling how the Free Masons had blackballed him, how the Odd Fellows had blackballed him, and how Christ had received him as he was. A great many orders and societies will not receive you, but I tell you, He will receive you, vile as you are—He, the Savior of sinners—He, the Redeemer of the lost world—He bids you come just as you are.

Ah, but there is another voice coming down from the gallery yonder: "I have intellectual difficulties; I cannot believe." A man came to me some time ago, and said, "I cannot." "Cannot what?" "Well," said he, "I cannot believe." "Who?" "Well," he repeated, "I cannot believe." "Who?" I asked. "Well, I can't believe myself." "Well, you don't want to." Make yourself out false every time, but believe in the truth of Christ. If a man says to me, "Mr. Moody, you have lied to me; you have dealt falsely with me," it may be so, but no man on the face of the earth can ever say that God ever dealt unfairly, or that He lied to him. If God says a thing, it is true. We don't ask you to believe in any man on the face of the earth, but we ask you to believe in Jesus Christ, who never lied—who never deceived anyone. If a man says he cannot believe Him, he says what is untrue.

"Ah, well, all those excuses don't apply to me," says another; "I can't feel." That is the very last excuse. When a man comes with [that] excuse, he is getting pretty near to the Lord.

We are having a body of men in England giving a new translation of the Scriptures. I think we should get them to put in a passage relating to feeling. With some people it is feel, feel, feel all the time. What kind of feeling have you got? Have you got a desire to be saved—have you got a desire to be present at the marriage supper? Suppose a gentleman asked me to dinner. I say, "I will see how I feel." "Sick?" he might ask. "No; it depends on how I feel." That is not the question—it is whether I will accept the invitation or not. The question with us is, will we accept salvation—will [we] believe? There is not a word about feelings in the Scriptures. When you come to your end, and you know that in a few days you will be in the presence of the Judge of all the earth, you will remember this excuse about feelings. You will be saying, "I went up to the tabernacle, I remember, and I felt very good, and before the meeting was over I felt very bad, and I didn't feel I had the right kind of feeling to accept the invitation." Satan will then say, "I made you feel so." Suppose you build your hopes and fix yourself upon the Rock of Ages, the devil cannot come to you. Stand upon the Word of God, and the waves of unbelief cannot touch you; the waves of persecution cannot assail you; the devil and all the fiends of hell cannot approach you if you only build your hopes upon God's Word. Say, "I will trust Him, though He slay me—I will take God at His word."

I haven't exhausted all the excuses. If I had you would make more before tomorrow morning. What has to be done with all the excuses is to bundle them all up and label them "Satan's lies." There is not an excuse but it is a lie. When you stand at the throne of God no man can give an excuse. If you have got a good excuse, don't give it up for anything I have said; don't give it up for anything your friend may have said. Take it up to the bar of God, and state it to Him; but if you have not got a good excuse—an excuse that will stand eternity—let it go tonight, and flee to the arms of a loving Savior.

It is easy enough to excuse yourself to hell, but you cannot excuse yourself to heaven. If you want an excuse, Satan will always find one ready for you. Accept the invitation now, my friends. Let your stores be closed till you accept this invitation; let your households go till you accept this invitation. Do not let the light come, do not eat, do not drink, till you accept the most important thing to you in this wide world. Will you stay tonight and accept this invitation? Don't make light of it. I can imagine some of you saying, "I never get so low as to make light of religion."

Suppose I get an invitation to dinner from a citizen of Chicago for tomorrow, and I don't answer it—I tear the invitation up. Would not that be making light of it? Suppose you pay no attention to the invitation tonight—is not that making light of it? Would anyone here be willing to write out an excuse something like this: "The tabernacle, October 29. To the King of heaven: While sitting in the tabernacle today, I received a very pressing invitation from one of your servants to sit at the marriage ceremony of the Son of God. I pray you have me excused." Is there a man or woman in this assembly would take their pen and write their name at the bottom of it? Is there a man or woman whose right hand would not forget its cunning, and whose tongue would not cleave to their mouth, if they were trying to do it? Well, you are doing this if you get up and go right out after you have heard the invitation. Who will write this: "To the Lord of lords and King of Glory: While sitting in the tabernacle this beautiful Sabbath evening, October 29, 1876, I received a pressing invitation from one of your servants to be present at the marriage supper. I hasten to accept." Will anyone sign this? Who will put their name to it? Is there not a man or woman saying, down deep in their soul, "By the grace of God I will sign it"; "I will sign it by the grace of God, and will meet that sainted mother who has gone there"; "I will sign and accept that invitation, and meet that loving wife or dear child." Are there not some here tonight who will accept that invitation?

I remember while preaching in Glasgow, an incident occurred which I will relate. I had been preaching there several weeks, and the night was my last one, and I pleaded with them as I had never pleaded there before. I urged those people to meet me in that land. It is a very solemn thing to stand before a vast audience for the last time, and think you may never have another chance of asking them to come to Christ. I told them I would not have another opportunity, and urged them to accept and just asked them to meet me at that marriage supper. At the conclusion, I soon saw a tall young lady coming into the inquiry room. She had scarcely come in when another tall young lady came in, and she went up to the first and put her arms round her and wept. Pretty soon another young lady came, and went up to the first two and just put her arms around them both. I went over to see what it was, and found that, although they had been sitting in different parts of the building, the sure arrow of conviction went down to their souls, and brought them to the inquiry room. Another young lady came down from the gallery, and said, "Mr. Moody, I want to become a Christian." I asked a young Christian to talk to her; and when she went home that night about ten o'clock—her mother was sitting up for her—she said, "Mother, I have accepted the invitation to be present at the marriage supper of the Lamb." Her mother and father laid awake that night talking about the salvation of the child. That was Friday night, and next day (Saturday) she was unwell, and before long her sickness developed into scarlet fever, and a few days after I got this letter:

Mr. Moody—Dear Sir: It is now my painful duty to [tell] you that the dear girl concerning whom I wrote to you on

Monday, has been taken away from us by death. Her departure, however, has been signally softened to us, for she told us yesterday she was "going home to be with Jesus"; and after giving messages to many, told us to let Mr. Moody and Mr. Sankey know that she died a happy Christian.

My dear sir, let us have your prayer that consolation and needed resignation and strength may be continued to us, and that our two dear remaining little ones may be kept in health if the Lord wills. I repeated a line of the hymn,

> In the Christian's home in glory,
> There remains a land of rest,

when she took it up at once, and tried to sing, "When the Savior's gone before to fulfill my soul's request." This was the last conscious thing she said. I should say that my dear girl also expressed a wish that the lady she conversed with on Friday evening should also know that she died a happy Christian.

When I heard this, I said to Mr. Sankey, "If we do nothing else we have been paid for coming across the Atlantic. There is one soul we have saved, whom we will meet on the resurrection morn."

Oh, my dear friends, are there not some here tonight who will decide this question? Do accept this invitation; let the sickness come, let sorrow come, you will be sure of meeting at the marriage supper of the Lamb. Blessed is he who shall be found at that marriage feast.

Daniel is one of the great Bible figures with which even the unchurched have some vague familiarity.

Moody gave few sermons dealing with biblical characters, but those characters he selected were particularly outstanding. Daniel displayed the attributes of a true man of God. Moody found in him the qualities that lent themselves to the needs of the day.

This three-part message begins with Daniel's life as a child in Babylon. His desire to remain separate from the pagan nation brings about many great opportunities for him. He is well-educated, and as a result of faithfulness to God, he is placed within the inner circle of important men in the Babylonian kingdom.

Throughout his life, Daniel remained a man of great devotion to God. This not only led to his rise in power, but he was also subjected to great persecution. Moody brings out the character and witness of Daniel and encourages the audience to see him as an example of what a Christian should be. Daniel is also used as a model of how to win souls, a common theme in Moody's preaching.

CHAPTER SEVEN

The Prophet Daniel

Part One

I want to talk about the life of the prophet Daniel. The word means "God [is my Judge] . . . ." Therefore, he had to report himself to God and hold himself responsible to Him. I do not know just what time Daniel went down to Babylon. I know that in the third year of King Jehoiakim, Nebuchadnezzar took ten thousand of the chief men of Jerusalem and carried them captive down to Babylon. I am glad these chief men who stirred on the war were given into the great king's hands. Unlike too many of the ringleaders in our great war, they got the punishment on their own heads. Among the captives were four young men. They had been converted doubtless under Jeremiah, the "weeping prophet" that God had sent to the children of Israel. Many had mocked at [Jeremiah] when he lifted up his voice against their sins. They had laughed at his tears and told him to his face, as many say of us, that he was getting up a false excitement.

But these four young men listened, and had the backbone to [stand up] for God.

And now, after they were [brought] to Babylon, the king said a number of the children should be educated, and ordered the same kind of meat and wine set before them that were used in his own palace, and that at the end of a year they should be brought before him. Daniel and his three friends were among these.

Now no young man ever comes to the city but has great temptation cross his path as he enters it. And just at this turning point in his life, as in Daniel's, must lie the secret of his success. If you see success in statesmen, in lawyers, or men in any walk in life, you ask the secret of it, and you find it in this same time of youth. Jacob turned away from God, and David turned away from God, but only just in proportion as they had not fully and entirely given themselves up to Him when they were young men.

Yes, that was the secret of this young man Daniel's success; he took his stand with God right on his entering the gate of Babylon and cried to God to keep him steadfast. And he needed to cry hard. A law of his and his nation's God was that no man should eat meat offered to idols; but now came the king's first edict, that this young man should eat the meat he himself did. I do not think it took young Daniel long to make up his mind. The law of God forbade it, and he would not do it. "He purposed in his heart"—in his heart, mark that—that he would not defile himself. He did not do it in his head, but love in his heart prompted him.

If some Chicago Christians could have advised Daniel, they'd have said, "Don't you do it; don't set aside the meat; that would be a species of Phariseeism. The moment you take your stand and say you won't eat it, you say in effect you are better than other people." That is the kind of talk too often heard now. Oh, yes, "When you are in Rome do as the Romans do"; they would have insisted to the poor young captive that he might, and ought to, carry out the commandments of his God when he was in his own country, but not there where he was a poor slave; he could not possibly carry along his religion down there to Babylon. Thank God, this young man said he would not eat, and ordering the meat taken away, got the eunuch to bring him [vegetables]. And behold, when he came before the king, the eunuch's fears were gone, for the faces of Daniel and the rest of the dear boys were fairer and fatter than any that the king looked down upon. They hadn't noses, like too many in our streets, as red as if they were just going to blossom. It is God's truth, and Daniel tested it, that cold water, with a clear conscience, is better than wine.

And the king one day had a dream, and all the wise men were called. But they all said, "We cannot interpret it; it is too hard." The king in wrath threatened them, and, still getting no answer, made an edict that all the wise men should be put to death. And the officers came to Daniel with the rest of the wise men, but Daniel was not afraid. I can imagine he prayed to God, falling low on his knees with his face to the earth, and asked Him what to do; and then he crawled into bed and slept like a child. We would hardly sleep well under such circumstances. And in his sleep God told him the meaning of the dream. There must have been joy among the wise men that one of their number had found it and that the king would save their lives. And he is brought before the king and cries out, "O king, while thou did'st lie with thy head on thy pillow, thou did'st dream, and in thy dream thou sawest a great image." I can imagine at these opening words how the king's eyes flashed, and how he cried out with joy, "Yes, that is it, the whole thing comes back to me now." And then Daniel, in a deathlike stillness, unfolds all the interpretation, and tells the king that the golden head of the great image represents his own government. I suppose Babylon was the biggest city ever in the world. It was sixty miles around. Some writers put the walls from sixty-five to eighty-five feet high, and twenty-five feet wide; four chariots could ride abreast on top of them. A street fifteen miles long divided the grand city, and hanging gardens in acres made the public parks. It was like Chicago—so flat that they had to resort to artificial mounds; and, again like Chicago, the products of vast regions flowed right into and through it.

This great kingdom, Daniel told the king, was his own; but he said a destroying kingdom should come, and afterward a third and fourth kingdom, when at the last, the God of heaven should set up His kingdom. And Daniel himself lived to see the first overthrown, when the Medes and Persians came in, and centuries after came Alexander, and then the Romans. I believe in the literal fulfillment, so far, of Daniel's God-given words, and in the sure fulfillment of the final prophecy of the "stone cut out of the mountains without hands," that by-and-by shall grind the kingdoms of this world into dust, and bring in the kingdom of peace. Then will be the millennium, and Christ will sway His scepter over all the earth. Well, the king was very much pleased. He gave [Daniel] a place near the throne, and he became one of the chief men of the world, and all his three friends were put in high office. God had blessed them signally, and he blessed them still more, and that was perhaps a harder thing—in keeping them true to Him in their prosperity. Their faith and fortunes waxed strong together.

Time went on, and [then there was] a crisis indeed. "Nebuchadnezzar, the king," we read, "made an image of gold, one hundred and ten feet high and nine feet wide." It was not gilded, but solid gold. When Babylon was pillaged the second time, a single god was found in the temple that was worth between two and three million pounds sterling. The king's monstrous image was set up in the plains of Dura, near to the city. I suppose he wanted to please his kingly vanity by inaugurating a universal religion. When the time came for the dedication, I do not suppose Daniel was there. He was perhaps in Egypt or some other province, on affairs of the empire. Counselors, satraps, high secretaries, and the princes of the people were ordered to hasten to the dedication, and when they should hear the sound of the cornet, flute, and psaltery announce that the great idol was consecrated, they were to bow down and worship it.

Perhaps they called the ceremony the unveiling of the monument, as we should say, but one command is certain, that at the given signal all the people were to fall to the earth in worship. But in the law of God there is something against that: "Thou shalt have no other gods but Me." God's law went right against the king's. Oh, would all of us have Daniel's three friends to do the right thing at any hazard! Would none of us, without backbone, have advised him to just bow down a little so that no one would notice it, or to merely bow down but not worship it! The hour came, and Daniel's friends refused to bow down. They refused utterly to bend the knee to a god of gold. How many cry out in this city, "Give me gold, give me money, and I will do anything." Such may think that men in Nebuchadnezzar's time should not bow down to a golden idol, but they themselves are every day doing just that very thing. Money is their golden image, or position, or golden ambition.

Well, the informers came to the king, and told him that Shadrach, Meshach, and Abednego had stood with unbended knee, and straightway they were hurried before him, the old king speechless with rage and gesturing his commands. I can imagine that one last chance was given them, after the king finally regained his voice, and that one of them, probably Meshach, spoke up in respectful but firm voice, that they must obey God rather than man. At once the raging king cried out, "What is your God that He can deliver you out of our hands?" And in the same breath screamed a command to bind them hand and foot and cast them into the fiery furnace, and make it seven times hotter than ever. The command was instantly executed, and the flames leaped out from the door and consumed the officers who cast them in.

But Jesus was with His servants as the flames wreathed about them, and soon word was brought to the king that four men walked about in the flames. Yes, they walked there with Jesus—they didn't run—as in a green pasture and beside still waters. And directly the king rushed up and cried, "Ye sons of the living God, come forth." And behold, even the hair of their heads was not singed. Then made the king a royal edict, that all in his realm should reverence the God of Meshach, Shadrach, and Abednego.

These glorious heroes braved even death because God was with them. Oh, friends, we want to be Christians with the same backbone; men and women who stand up for the right, and never mind what the world may say. I believe, before God, there would be ten thousand conversions in Chicago in the next twenty-four hours had we only a perfect consecration. God grant it us out of the abundance of His grace. I cannot go on now, but will finish about Daniel next Sunday morning.

Part Two

Last Sunday morning, we got to the second dream of King Nebuchadnezzar. This morning we will just take up where we broke off. The king had a dream, and he was greatly troubled. This time the particulars of the dream had not gone from him. They stood out vivid and clear in his mind as he sent out to fetch the wise men, and [he] called to them to give him the interpretation. But they could not give it.

When [the king] had his first dream he had summoned these same soothsayers, but they had stood silent. And now they stood silent again as the second dream was told them; they could not interpret it.

Once again he sends for the prophet Daniel that he had named after one of his gods, Belteshazzar. And the young prophet comes before the king, and as quick as the king sees him he feels sure that he will not get the meaning. Calling out from his throne, he tells how he had dreamed a dream, wherein he saw a tree in the midst of the earth, with branches that reached to heaven and the sight thereof to the ends of the earth; the beasts of the field had shelter under it, and the fowls of the air dwelt in the boughs thereof; and the tree was very fair and had much fruit, and all flesh was fed on it. And then, lowering his voice, he tells how, as he gazed, he saw a watcher and a holy one come down from heaven, who cried aloud, "Hew down the tree." "And now," cries the king, "can you tell me the interpretation?" And for a time Daniel stands still and motionless. Does his heart fail him? The record simply says, that "for one hour he was astonished." The ready words doubtless rush to his lips, but he hates to let them out; he doesn't want to tell how the king's kingdom and mind are going to depart from him, and he is to wander forth to eat grass like a beast. The king, too, hesitates; a dark foreboding for a time gets the better of curiosity. But, directly, he nerves himself to hear the worst, and speaks very kindly, "Do not be afraid to tell me, oh, Daniel; let not the dream or its interpretation trouble thee." And at last Daniel speaks, "O king, thou art the man; God has exalted thee over every king, and over all the world, but thou shalt be brought low; thou shalt be driven out from men and eat grass among the beasts of the field; but thy kingdom—as the great watcher spared the stump of the tree—shall afterwards return to thee. Wherefore, O king, break off thy sins by righteousness and thine iniquities by showing mercy to the poor, if it may be a lengthening of thy tranquility."

And straightway the king repented in sackcloth and

ashes, and so God [averted] the doom. But twelve months from that time Nebuchadnezzar was walking in his palace and boasting, "Is not this my great Babylon that I have built by the might of my power and for the honor of my majesty?" And behold while he yet spake, a voice came from heaven, saying, "Thy kingdom hath departed," and undoubtedly God then touched his reason, and straightway he ran madly through the gates to eat grass.

But his kingdom had not passed from him forever, and, according to the prophet's word, at the end of seven years, or possibly seven months, his reason came back, and he returned to his palace, and all his princes and officers gathered about him. Then immediately he sent out a new proclamation, and its closing words show his repentance and how Daniel had brought this mighty king to God.

> And at the end of the days I Nebuchadnezzar lifted up mine eyes unto heaven, and mine understanding returned unto me, and I blessed the Most High, and I praised and honoured him that liveth for ever, whose dominion is an everlasting dominion, and his kingdom is from generation to generation. . . .
>
> At the same time my reason returned unto me; and for the glory of my kingdom, mine honour and brightness returned unto me; and my counsellors and my lords sought unto me; and I was established in my kingdom, and excellent majesty was added unto me.
>
> Now I, Nebuchadnezzar, praise and extol . . . the King of heaven, all whose works are truth, and his ways judgment: and those that walk in pride he is able to abase *(Dan. 4:34, 36, 37)*.

And then he passes from the stage; This is the last record of him; and undoubtedly he and Daniel now walk the crystal pavement together. Oh, that mighty monarch was led to the God of the Hebrews by the faith of this Hebrew slave, and just because he had a religion and dared to make it known.

But now we lose sight of the prophet for a few years, perhaps fifteen or twenty. The next we hear is that Belshazzar was on the throne, possibly as regent. He was believed to have been a grandson of Nebuchadnezzar. One day he said he would make Daniel the third ruler of the people if he would tell him the handwriting on the wall. He was probably second himself, and Daniel would be next to him. Of this prince we have only one glimpse. The feast scene is the first and last we have of him, and it is enough. It was a great feast, and fully a thousand of his lords sat down together. Feasts in those days sometimes lasted six months. How long this one lasted we don't know. The king caroused with his princes and satraps and all the mighty men of Babylon, drinking and rioting and praying to gods of silver and gold and brass and stubble; just what we're doing today, if we bow the knee to the gods of this world. And the revelers, waxing wanton, even went into the temple and lay sacrilegious hands on the sacred vessels brought away from Jerusalem, and drank out of them, drank toasts to idols and harlots. And undoubtedly as they [were] drinking, they scoffed at the God of Israel. I see them swearing and rioting when—the king turns pale and trembles from head to foot. Above the golden candlesticks, on a bare space on the wall, he sees the writing of the God of Zion. He distinctly sees the terrible finger. His voice shakes with terror, but manages to falter out, "Bring in the wise men; any man that can read the handwriting I will make third ruler of the kingdom." And they come trooping in, but there is no answer, none of them can read it. They are skilled in Chaldean lore, but this [stumps] them. At last the queen comes in and whispers, "O king, there is one man in the kingdom who can read that writing; when your grandfather could not interpret his dreams he sent for Daniel the Hebrew, and he knew all about them. Can we not find him?"

And they find him, and now we see the man of God again standing before a king's throne. To the king's hurried promises of gifts and honors, he replies, "You can keep your rewards," and quietly turns his eyes on the writing. And he reads it at the first glance, for it is his Father's handwriting. *"Mene,"* he says, "thy kingdom hath departed from thee"; *"tekel:* thou art weighed in the balance and found wanting." Oh, sinner, what if God should put you in the balance, and you have not got Christ in your soul? How that word of doom must have rung through the palace that night! *"Upharsin:* thy kingdom is divided, it is given over to the hands of the enemy."

And the destruction did not tarry. The king recovered himself, banished his fears, the dream, and its interpretation as idle, and he went on drinking in his hall. He thought he was perfectly secure. He thought the great walls of Babylon perfectly safe. But Darius was besieging the city. The enemy was right upon him. Was that safe?

Oh, sinners of Chicago, death and hell are right on you! Death and hell, I say . . . are just as close, maybe, as the slayer's sword to those midnight revelers. While they reveled, the river Euphrates, that flowed under the walls, was turned into another channel; the hosts of Medes and Persians rushed through, unobstructed, and in a few minutes more battered down the king's gate and broke through the palace guard into the inmost palace chamber. And the king was slain, and his blood flowed in that banquet hall.

We are next told Darius took the throne and set over the people one hundred twenty rulers, and over these three presidents, of whom Daniel was first. And so we find him in office again. I do not know how long he was in that position. But by-and-by a conspiracy took [hold] among his fellow officers to get rid of him. They got jealous and said, "Let's see if we can't get this man removed; he's bossed us long enough, the sanctimonious old Hebrew." And then he was so impracticable, they couldn't do anything with him. There were plenty of collectors and treasurers, but he kept such a close eye on them that they only made their salaries. There was no plundering of the government with Daniel at the head. He was president of the princes, and all revenue accounts passed before him. I can overhear the plotters whispering, "If we can only put him out of the way, we can make enough in two or three years to retire from office, have a city house in Babylon, and two or three villas in the country, have enough for all our days, we can go down to Egypt and see something of the world; as things are now we can only get our exact dues, and it will take years to get anything respectable—yes, let's down with this pious Jew." Well, they worked things so as to get an investigating committee, hoping to catch him in his accounts. But they found no occasion nor fault against him. If he had put any relatives in office it would have been found out; if he had been guilty of speculation, or in any way broken the unalterable statutes of the kingdom, it would have come to light. Oh, what a bright light was that, standing alone in that great city for God and the majesty of law!

But at last they struck on one weak point, they called it—he would worship no one but the God of Israel. The law of his God was his only assailable side. "If we can only get Darius," the conspirators plotted, "to forbid anyone making a request for thirty days except from the king himself, we shall trap him, and then can cast him among the lions; we will take good care to have the lions hungry." And the hundred and twenty princes took long counsel together. "Take care," they said; "you must draw up the paper which is to be signed by the king with a deal of care and discretion. The king loves [Daniel], and he has influence. Don't speak of the movement outside of this meeting; it might come to the ears of the king, and we must talk to the king ourselves." When the [proposal] was all ready, the hundred and twenty princes came to the king and opened their business with flattering speech.

If people come to praise me, I know they've something else coming—they've got a purpose for telling me I am a good man. And so we naturally hear these men saying, "King Darius, live forever." They tell him how prosperous the realm is, and how much the people think of him. And then they tell him, in the most plausible manner that ever was, that if he would be remembered by children's children to all ages, just to sign this decree; it would be a memorial of his greatness and goodness forever. And the king replies graciously, "What is the decree you wish me to sign?" and, casting his eye over the paper, goes on, "I don't see any objection to that." In the pleasure of granting a request he thinks nothing of Daniel, and the princes carefully refrain from jogging his memory. And he asks for his signet ring and gives the royal stamp.

The edict has become one of the laws of the Medes and Persians, that alter not; it reads, "Any man that worships any God but me for thirty days shall be cast into the lions' den." The news spreads all through the city; it comes out perhaps in the Babylon *Inter-ocean*, and quickly gets to the ears of Daniel. I can imagine some of them going to the prophet and advising him about the edict. "If you can only get out of the way for a little time, if you can just quit Babylon for thirty days, it will advance your own and the public interest together. You are the chief secretary and treasurer, in fact you are the chief ruler in the government; you are an important man, and can do as you please. Well, now, just you get out of Babylon. Or, if you will stay in Babylon, don't let them catch you on your knees; at all events, don't pray at the window toward Jerusalem. If you will pray, close that window and pull down the curtain, and put something in the keyhole."

How many young men there are who don't dare to pray before their roommates; they've no moral courage. How many young men say to me, "Mr. Moody, don't ask me to get down on my knees at this prayer meeting." They want moral courage. Oh, thousands of men have been lost for want of moral courage, to dare to get down on their knees and pray to God. The idea of policy coming in here is all wrong. I can imagine how that old prince, Daniel, now in his gray hair, would view such a thought, that he is going to desert his God in his old age. All the remonstrances that must have been made fell dead; he just went on praying as usual three times a day, with his face toward Jerusalem. Our businessmen, too many of them, "don't have any time to pray," business is so pressing. But this old prophet found plenty of time, though secretary and treasurer of the most important empire in the world. And, besides his own business, he had to attend, doubtless, to much belonging by right to those hundred and twenty. But he would never have been too busy or ashamed at a prayer meeting to stand up for God. He had a purpose, and he dared to make it known. He knew whom he worshipped. The idea of looking back to church records of years ago to see whether a man has professed religion is all wrong. In Babylon they knew whom Daniel believed in; these hundred and twenty knew the very day after the passing of the edict.

[Daniel] knows they are watching near his window when the hour comes for prayer. He can see two men close at his side, and knows they are spies; perhaps they may be taking down every word he says for the papers. The moment comes, and he falls on his knees, and in tones louder than ever makes his prayer to the God of Israel, Abraham, Isaac, and Jacob. He doesn't omit to pray for the king. (It is right to pray for our rulers. If we quit praying for our rulers, our country will go to pieces. The reason they are not better, oftentimes, is just because we do not pray for them.) And now the spies rush to the king and say, "O Darius, live forever; do you know there is a man in your kingdom that won't obey you?" "Won't obey me! Who is he?" "Why, that man Daniel." And the king says, "I know he won't bow down and worship me; I know that he worships the God of heaven." Then the king sets his heart to deliver him all the day from the hands of those one hundred and twenty men. But they come to him and say, "If you want to break your law your kingdom will depart, your subjects will no longer obey you; you must deliver him to the lions' den."

And Darius is compelled, and at last gives the word to have him sent away and cast into the lions' den, and these men take good care to have the den filled with the hungriest beasts in Babylon. He is thrown headlong into the den, but the angel of God flies down, and [Daniel] lights unharmed on the bottom. The lions' mouths are stopped. They are as harmless as lambs. The old prophet at the [usual] hour drops on his knees and prays with his face towards Jerusalem, as calmly as in his chamber. And when it gets late, he just lays his head on one of the lions and goes to sleep, and undoubtedly no one in all Babylon slept sweeter than Daniel in the lions' den.

In the palace the king cannot sleep. He orders his chariot, and early in the morning rattles over the pavement and jumps down at the lions' den. I see him alight from his chariot in eager haste, and hear him cry down through the mouth of the den, "Oh, Daniel, servant of the living God, is thy God whom thou reverest continually, able to deliver thee from the lions?" Hark! Why, it is a resurrection voice! It is Daniel saying, "My God is able; He hath sent one of his angels and hath shut the lions' mouths." I can see them now just embrace each other, and together they jump into the chariot and away they go back to the palace to breakfast.

Part Three

I want to say some further things about Daniel. I want to refer to how an angel came to him, and, as we read in the twelfth chapter of Daniel, told him he was a man greatly beloved. Another angel had come to him with the same message. It is generally thought this last angel was the same one spoken of in Revelation, first chapter, thirteenth verse, as coming to John when banished at the Isle of Patmos. People thought he was sent off there alone; but no; the angel of God was with him. And so with Daniel. Here in the tenth chapter and fifth verse he says, "Then I lifted up mine eyes, and behold, a certain man clothed with fine linen, and otherwise arrayed as God's messenger, who cried, 'Oh, Daniel, a man greatly beloved, understand the words which I speak unto thee, and stand upright, for unto thee am I now sent.' " It was Daniel's need that brought him from the glory land. It was the Son of God right by his side in that strange land. And that was the second time that the word came to him that he was greatly beloved. Yes, three times a messenger came from the throne of God to tell him this.

I love to speak of that precious verse in the eleventh chapter, the thirty-second verse: "The people that do know their God shall be strong, and do exploits," and also of the twelfth chapter and second and third verses: "And many of them that sleep in the dust of the earth shall awake, some to everlasting life, and some to shame and everlasting contempt; and they that be wise shall shine as the brightness of the firmament; and they that turn many to righteousness as the stars for ever and ever."

This was the angel's comfort to Daniel, and a great comfort it was. The fact with all of us is that we like to shine. There is no doubt about that. Every mother likes her child to shine. If her boy shines at school by getting to the head of his class, the proud mother tells all the neighbors, and she has a right to. But it is not the great of this world that will shine the brightest. For a few years they may shed bright light, but they go out in darkness, without an inner light. Supplying the brightness they go out in black darkness.

Where are the great men who did not know Daniel's God? Did they shine long? Why, we know of Nebuchadnezzar and the rest of them scarcely a thing, except as they fill in the story about these humble men of God. We are not told that statesmen shall shine; they may for a few years or days, but they are soon forgotten. Look at those great ones who passed away in the days of Daniel. How wise in counsel they were, how mighty and victorious over hundreds of nations. What gods upon earth they were! Yet their names are forgotten and written in the grave. So-called philosophers—do they live? Behold men of science—scientific men they call themselves—going down into the bowels of the earth, digging away at some carcass and trying to make it talk against the voice of God. They shall go down to death by-and-by, and their names shall rot. But the man of God shines. Yes, he it is who shall shine as the stars forever and ever. This Daniel has been gone for 2,500 years, but still increasing millions read of his life and actions. And so it shall be to the end; he will only get better known and better loved; he shall only shine the brighter as the world grows older. Of a truth, they that be wise and turn many to righteousness shall shine on, like stars to eternity.

And this blessed, thrice blessed, happiness, like all the blessings of God's kingdom, is for everyone. Even without the first claim to education or refinement you can shine if you will. One of you sailors there can shine forever if you only go to work for the kingdom. The Bible doesn't say the great shall shine but they that turn many to righteousness.

A false impression has got hold of many of God's people. They have the idea that only a few can talk about God's affairs. Nine-tenths of the people say, if anything is to be done for the souls of men, "Oh, the ministers must do it." It doesn't enter into the heart of the people that they have any part in the matter. It is the devil's work to keep Christians from the blessed luxury of winning souls to God. Anyone can do this work. A little girl only eleven years old came to me in a Sunday school and said, "Won't you please pray that God will make me a winner of souls?" I felt so proud of her, and my pride was justified, for she has become one of the best winners of souls in this country. Oh, suppose she lives threescore years, and goes on winning four or five souls every year; at the end of her journey there will be three hundred souls on the way to glory. And how long will it be before that little company swells to a great army. Don't you see how that little mountain [brook] keeps swelling till it carries everything before it? Little trickling streams have run into it, till now, a mighty river, it has great cities on its banks, and the commerce of all nations floating on its waters. So when a single soul is won to Christ you cannot see the result. A single one multiplies to a thousand and that into ten thousand. Perhaps a million shall be the fruit; we cannot tell. We only know that the Christian who has turned so many to righteousness shall indeed shine forever and ever. Look at those poor fishermen, Jesus' disciples, how unlettered. They were not learned men, but great in winning souls. So [there is] not a child here but can work for God.

The one thing that keeps people from work is that they don't have the desire. If a man has this desire God soon qualifies him. And what we want is God's qualification; it must come from Him. I have been thinking what shall be done for the next thirty days that I continue to preach here. If I should just put it to vote, and asked all Christians who wanted prayers to rise, all of you, I know, would rise. There are at least three thousand Christians here. Now, is it too much to ask that three thousand Christians will each lead one soul to Christ this coming week? The Son of God died on the cross for you. Right here in this tabernacle you can tell those weeping over their sins about God and heaven. How many times I have watched, just to see if Christians would speak to these sorrowing ones! If we only had open-eyed watchers for souls, there wouldn't be a night but five hundred or a thousand inquirers would crowd into the inquiry rooms. These anxious inquirers are at every meeting, just waiting to have warm-hearted Christians bring them to Christ. They are timid, but will always listen to one speaking to them about Christ. Suppose each one of you now prayed, "Give me some soul this week for my hire." What would be the result? This room would not hold the multitude sending up shouts of praise to God and making heaven glad. Where there is an anxious sinner there is the place for the Christian.

A little bed-ridden boy I knew kept mourning that he couldn't work for Jesus. The minister told him to pray, and pray he did; and the persons he prayed for one by one felt the load of their sins and professed Christ. When he heard that such a one had not given in, he just turned his face to the wall and prayed harder. Well, he died, [and] by his little memorandum it was found that he had prayed for fifty-six persons daily by name, and before he was buried all of them had given their hearts to Jesus. Tell me that little boy won't shine in the kingdom of God! These little ones can be used by God.

I remember a good many years ago I resolved I wouldn't let a day pass without talking to someone about their soul's salvation. And it was in that school God qualified me to speak the gospel. If we [are] faithful over small things God will promote us. If God says, "Speak to that young man," obey the word, and you will be given by-and-by plenty of souls. I went down past the corner of Clark and Lake streets one day, and, fulfilling my vow, on seeing a man leaning up against a lamppost, I went up to him and said, "Are you a Christian?" He damned me and cursed me and said to mind my own business. He knew me, but I didn't know him. He said to a friend of his that afternoon that he had never been so insulted in his life, and he told him to say to me that I was damning the cause I pretended to represent. Well, the friend came and delivered his message. "Maybe I am doing more hurt than good," I said; "maybe I am mistaken and God hasn't shown me the right way." That was the time I was sleeping and living in the Young Men's Christian Association rooms, where I was then president, secretary, janitor, and everything else. Well, one night after midnight I heard a knock at the door. And there on the step leading into the street stood this stranger I had made so mad at the lamppost, and he said he wanted to talk to me about his soul's salvation. He said, "Do you remember the man you met about three months ago at a lamppost, and how I cursed you? I have had no peace since that night, I couldn't sleep. Oh, tell me what to do to be saved." And we just fell down on our knees, and I prayed, and that day he went to the noon prayer meeting and openly confessed the Savior, and soon after went to the war a Christian man. I do not know but he died on some southern battlefield or in a hospital, but I expect to see him in the kingdom of God. Oh, how often have I thanked God for that word to that dying sinner that He put into my mouth!

And I have just been engaged in this personal work all my life. God's business is not to be done wholesale. Think of the Master Himself talking just to Nicodemus and then how He talked to that poor woman at the well of Samaria. Christ's greatest utterances were delivered to congregations of one or two. How many are willing to speak to tens of thousands but not to speak to a few! I knew a man who was going to get rich and do large things for God but he never did anything; he wouldn't do little things—that was the secret. Oh, be willing, Christians, to be built into the temple, as a polished capstone, or just a single brick—no matter just how, but somehow. Say to yourself in your home, in your Sunday school classes, in your daily rounds, "I'll not let this sun go down till I lead one soul to Christ." And then, having done all, shall you shine as gems in the great white throne forever and ever.

I want to tell you how I got the first impulse to work solely for the conversion of men. For a long time after my conversion I didn't accomplish anything. I hadn't got into my right place; that was it. I hadn't thought enough of this personal work. I'd get up in prayer meeting, and I'd pray with the others, but just to go up to a man and take hold of his coat and get him down on his knees, I hadn't yet got around to that. It was in 1860 the change came. In the Sunday school I had a pale delicate young man as one of the teachers. I knew his burning piety, and assigned him to the worst class in the school. They were all girls, and it was an awful class. They kept gadding around in the schoolroom and were laughing and carrying on all the while. And this young man had better success than anyone else. One Sunday he was absent, and I tried myself to teach the class, but [I] couldn't do anything with them; they seemed farther off than ever from any concern about their souls. Well, the day after his absence, early Monday morning, the young man came into the store where I worked, and, tottering and bloodless, [he] threw himself down on some boxes. "What's the matter?" I said. "I have been bleeding at the lungs, and they have given me up to die," he said. "But you are not afraid to die?" I questioned. "No," said he. "I am not afraid to die, but I have got to stand before God and give an account of my stewardship, and not one of my Sabbath school scholars has been brought to Jesus. I have failed to bring one, and haven't any strength to do it now." He was so weighed down that I got a carriage and took that dying man in it, and we called at the homes of every one of his scholars, and to each one he said, as best his faint voice would let him, "I have come to just ask you to come to the Savior," and then he prayed as I never heard before. And for ten days he labored in that way, sometimes walking to the nearest houses. And at the end of that ten days every one of that large class had yielded to the Savior. Full well I remember the night before he went away (for the doctors said he must hurry to the south), how we held a true lovefeast. It was the very gate of heaven, that meeting. He prayed and prayed; he didn't ask them, he didn't think they could pray; and then we sang, "Blessed Be the Tie That Binds." It was a beautiful night in June that he left on the Michigan Southern, and I was down to the train to help him off. And every one [of] those girls gathered there again, all unknown to each other; and the depot seemed a second gate to heaven, in the joyful, yet tearful, communion and farewells between those newly redeemed souls and him whose crown of rejoicing it will be that he led them to Jesus. At last the gong sounded, and, supported on the platform, the dying man shook hands with each one and whispered, "I will meet you yonder."

Some of the very best, most constant teachers I had before going to Europe were converted at that time, and they, in their turn, have gathered many sheaves, and I myself was led by this incident, this wonderful blessing of God on individual effort, to throw up my business and give my whole strength to God's work.

Shall not that young man have a high place, a place very near the Savior of men, in the day when He makes up His jewels? Oh, friends, if you want to shine in the kingdom of God, work for Him today. Shall we not, every one, go out of this building saying, "I will try to bring one soul to Christ today?"

Blindness comes in physical and spiritual varieties. In this message, Moody describes how spiritual blindness has been placed upon humanity by the devil for the purpose of hiding the gospel.

Moody uses the analogy of physical blindness very effectively, showing that it is very similar to spiritual blindness. However, unlike physical sightlessness, there is hope of recovery for those without spiritual vision.

Several forms of blindess exist: greed, work, ambition, pleasure, fashion, and alcohol prevent those afflicted from coming to Christ. Illustrations abound, giving the sermon extra power in touching many hearts, giving them a chance to see their dilemma and do something about it.

CHAPTER EIGHT

Spiritual Blindness

You who have been here during the week have heard me speaking on the fourth chapter of Luke and the eighteenth verse. I spoke on the first three clauses of that verse, and we have now come to the next clause, in which He tells us that He came to give sight to the blind—for the recovery of sight to the blind. Paul tells us, in his second epistle to the Corinthians, fourth chapter, third and fourth verse,

> But if our gospel be hid, it is hid to them that are lost; in whom the god of this world hath blinded the minds of them which believe not, lest the light of the glorious gospel of Christ, who is the image of God, should shine unto them.

"If the gospel be hid, . . . in whom the god of this world hath blinded." This world is just one large blind asylum—it is full of blind people. Last Wednesday night I tried to tell you that the world was full of broken hearts; last night I tried to tell you that the world was full of captives, bound hand and foot in sin, and tonight I tell you that it is full of blind people. Not only blind people, but they are bound and brokenhearted. You might say that nearly all those in the world come under [those] three headings.

Now just look at the contrast between Satan and Christ. Satan breaks men's hearts. But Christ binds them up. Satan binds the people of this earth hand and foot, but Christ breaks the fetters and sets them free; Satan makes us blind, but Christ opens our eyes. He came to do this, and just see how He was received. He went into that synagogue at Nazareth and preached this glorious gospel, and commenced by telling them that the spirit of the Lord was upon Him. He went on to tell them that He had come to save them; and what did they do? They thrust Him out of the city and took Him to the brow of the hill, and they would have hurled Him into hell if they could. And men have been as bitter toward the gospel all along these eighteen hundred years. Why, some men would tear the preacher of it limb from limb if it wasn't for the law.

Then we find when He goes to Bethany, and raises up the brother of Martha and Mary and binds up broken hearts as He goes along and preaches mercy, that they want to kill Him. We find Him in the third chapter of Mark setting the captive free. Here we find a man possessed of demons, whom no one could cure, set at liberty by the Son of man, and because they lost a few swine in the healing, they told Him to depart from their coasts. Then we find Him just a few days before His death, almost on His way to Calvary, giving sight to that blind man. And for all this they take him to that mount and nail him to a cross. Oh what blindness!

We are told that there are 3,000,000 people in the world who are called blind. Everyone calls them blind because they haven't their natural sight. But do you ever think how many are spiritually blind in this world? Why, if there are 3,000,000 people in the world who have not their natural sight, how many do you suppose are spiritually blind? We sympathize with those who have lost their sight. Nothing appeals to our sympathy so readily. I believe I could raise thousands of dollars among you by telling you about some blind one who is suffering for the necessities of life through his affliction. How many of you wouldn't put your hand in your pockets and give liberally? How it moves our compassion—how it moves our hearts as we see blind men, women, or children in the streets. How your heart goes out to those poor unfortunates.

I was at a meeting in London, and I heard a man speaking with wonder, but power and earnestness. "Who is that man?" I asked, my curiosity being excited. "Why, that is Dr.———. He is blind." I felt some interest in this man, and at the close of the meeting I sought an interview, and he told me that he had been stricken blind when very young. His mother took him to a doctor and asked him about his sight. "You must give up all hope," the doctor said. "Your boy is blind, and will be forever." "What, do you think my boy will never see?" asked his mother. "Never again." The mother took her boy to her bosom and cried, "Oh, my boy, who will take care of you when I am gone—who will look [after] you!" Forgetting the faithfulness of that God she had [taught] him to love. He became a servant of the Lord, and was permitted to print the Bible in twelve different languages, printed in the raised letters, so that all blind people could read the Scriptures themselves. He had a congregation, my friends, of 3,000,000 people, and I think that blind man was one of the happiest beings in all London. He was naturally blind, but he had eyes to his soul, and could see a bright eternity in the future. He had built his foundation upon the living God.

We pity those who have not their natural sight; but how you should pity yourself if you are spiritually blind. If we could get all the spiritually blind in this city! You talk about those great political meetings, they would be nothing to the crowd you would collect. Why, just look at all the men in this city who are blind, and many of them are in the churches. This has been the trouble with men always. Christ couldn't get men to understand they were blind; He couldn't even get His disciples to open their eyes until after He went up to heaven. And then they received the spiritual truth. How many are the professed children of God we read of in the book of Revelation?

I think tonight I might pick up some of the different classes who are blind. I am somewhat acquainted with the rich men of this city, and I don't think it would take long to prove that the leading men of this city are blind—blind to their own interests. Take a man just spending all his strength and energies to get money. He is money blind. He is so blind in his pursuit that he cannot see the God of heaven. Money is his god. His cry is continually "Money, money," and it is the cry of many here in Chicago. They don't care about God, don't care about salvation, don't heed their eternal condition so long as they get money, money, money. And a great many of them have got it. But how lean their souls are. God has given them the desire of their heart, but He has given them leanness of soul.

I heard of a man who had accumulated great wealth. And death came upon him suddenly, and he realized, as the saying is, that "there was no bank in the shroud," that he couldn't take anything away with him; we may have all the money on earth, but we must leave it behind us. He called a lawyer in and commenced to will away his property before he went away. His little girl couldn't understand exactly where he was going, and she said, "Father, have you got a home in that land you are going to?" The arrow went down to his soul. "Got a home there?" The rich man had hurled away God, and neglected to secure a home there for the sake of his money, and he found it was now too late. He was money mad, and he was money blind. It wouldn't be right for me to give names, but I could tell you a good many here in Chicago who are going on in this way—spending all their lives in the accumulation of what they cannot take with them. This is going on while many poor people are suffering for the necessities of life. These men don't know they are blind—money is their god.

There is another class who don't care so much for money. We might call them business blind. It is business, business, business with them all the time. In the morning they haven't time to worship. They must attend to business; must get down to the store. Down they run, and haven't time to get home to dinner. They mustn't let anyone get ahead of them; and they get home late at night, and their families have gone to bed. They scarcely ever see their children. It is all business with them.

A man told me not long ago, "I must attend to my business. That is my first consideration, and see that none gets ahead of me." That is his god. I don't care if he is an elder or a deacon in the church. [Business] is his god. The god of business has blinded him. Look at the merchant prince who died the other day. Men called him a clever, shrewd man. Call that shrewdness—to pile up wealth for a lifetime and leave no record behind so that we know he has gone to heaven? He rose above men in his business; he devoted his whole soul to it, and the world called him a power among men; the world called him great. But let the Son of God write his obituary; let Him put an epitaph on his tombstone, and it would be, "Thou fool." Man says, "I must attend to business first"; God says, "Seek first the kingdom of God." I don't care what your business may be; it may be honorable, legitimate, and all that, and you think you must attend to it first; bear in mind that God tells every man to seek His kingdom first.

There is another class of people who are blind. They don't care so much about riches, they are not very ambitious to become rich, they don't spend their lives in business matters. They are politically blind. They are mad over politics; they are bound up in the subject. There will be a great many broken hearts in a week hence. They have got their favorite candidate to attend to and they cannot find time to worship God. How little prayer there has been about the election. There has been a good deal of work, but how much praying has been done? We want prayer to go up all over our land that high and honest men may rule over us. But they are so excited over this election that they have no time to pray to the God of heaven. They are politically blind. How many men within our recollection, who have set their hearts upon the Presidential chair, have gone down to the grave with disappointment? They were poor, blind men, and the world called them great. Oh, how foolish; how blind. They didn't seek God; they only sought one thing— greatness—position and office. They were great, brilliant, clever men, but when they were summoned into the presence of their God, what a wreck. Men so brilliant might have wielded an influence for the Son of God that would have lived in the hearts of the people for generations to come, and the streams of their goodness might have flowed long after they went to heaven. But they lived for the world, and their works went to dust.

But a great number of people don't care for business or politics, they only want a little money so as to get pleasure. How many men have been blinded by pleasure. A lady told me in the inquiry room she would like to become a Christian, but there was a ball coming on, and she didn't want to become a Christian until after the ball. The ball was worth more then to her than the kingdom of God. For this ball she would put off the kingdom of God until it was over, forgetting that death might come to her in the meantime and usher her into the presence of God. How blind she was, and many are just like her. The kingdom of God is offered to them without

money and without price, and yet for a few days of pleasure they forfeit heaven and everything dear to their eternity.

I was talking to a lady who, with the tears running
down her cheeks upon my speaking to her, said, "The
fact is, if I become a Christian I have to give up all pleasure. I cannot go to a theater; I cannot read any novels; I
cannot play cards. I have nothing else to do." Oh, what
blindness! Look at the pleasure of being taken into the
Lord's vineyard, and the joy and luxury of working for
Him and leading souls to Christ. And people with their
eyes wide open would rather bend down to the god of
pleasure than become Christians.

Then there is the god of fashion. How many women
just devote their lives to it. They want to see the last bon-
net, the last cloak, the last dress. They can't think of anything else. Said a lady to me, "I am always thinking of
fashion; it doesn't matter if I get down on my knees to
pray, I am always thinking of a new dress." You may
laugh at this, but it's true. Pleasure in the ballroom and
fashion is the god of a great many people. Oh, that we
may lift our eyes to something nobler. Suppose you don't
have so many dresses and give something to the poor,
you will have something then which will give you joy and
comfort that will last you always. I pity the man or
woman who lives for the day like the butterfly—those
whose minds are fixed upon fashion and pleasure, and
have no time to look to their perishing souls. A good
many people don't know they are [blind].

Look at that young man. You call him a fast young
man. He has got a salary of one thousand dollars, and it
costs him three thousand dollars to live. Where does he
get the money? Where does it come from? His father
cannot give it to him because he is poor. His employer
begins to get suspicious. "I only give him one thousand
dollars a year, and he is living at the rate of three thousand dollars. By-and-by he looks into his account book

and finds it overdrawn. Thus he is ruined—character blasted. Oh, how many are of this stamp in Chicago? It is only a question of time. How many young men have we got living beyond their income—taking money out of their employer's drawer. They say, "Well, I am going to the theater tonight, and I will just take a dollar; I will put it back next week." But when next week comes, he hasn't put it back and takes another dollar. He has taken two dollars now. He keeps on draw, draw, drawing, when by-and-by it all comes out. He loses his place, doesn't get any letters of recommendation, and the poor man is ruined. My friends, this is not the description of an isolated case. This class is all over the country. I wish I could send you the letters I get about just such cases. I got one the other day from a young mother with a family of beautiful children. She told me how happy they had lived—husband, wife, and children, and how one night her husband came home excited, his face white with terror, and said, "I've got to fly from justice. Goodbye." He has gone from her, and she said it seemed as if she could die; her husband disgraced and starving couldn't get anything to do. Her cry seemed to be "Help, help me." Is not the country full of such cases? Is it not blindness and madness for men to go on in this way? If anyone is here tonight following in the way of these men, I pray God your eyes may be opened before you are led to death and ruin.

You know we had a full meeting today, and the subject was "Intemperance." How many young men are there who spend their time in the saloons of the city? I am afraid many will be led astray next Tuesday. I always dread an election day—I generally see so many young men beastly drunk. They are led away, and that is another quick road down to hell. May the young men see the folly of this, and on that day stand firm. May God open your eyes. How many young men are there whose characters have been blasted by strong drink? How many brilliant men in the Chicago bar have gone down to death by it? Some of the noblest statesmen, some of the most brilliant orators and men of all professions have been borne down to the drunkard's grave. May God open your eyes to show the folly of tampering with strong drink.

Now, many men say, "I am not going down to the grave of a drunkard." They think they have strength to stop when they like. When it gets hold, there is nothing within us by which we can save ourselves. He alone can give you power to resist the cup of temptation. He alone can give you power to overcome its influence, if you only will believe Him. The god of this world has been trying to make you believe that a man can do it himself, and Christ will have nothing to do with him. The god of this world is a liar. I come with authority to tell you—I don't care how far gone you are; don't care how blessed you may be—that the Son of God can and will save you if you only believe Him. If there is one here tonight under the power of strong drink come [to Him] tonight. We lift up our voice to warn you.

Look at that man in a boat on Niagara River. He is only about a mile from the rapids. A man on the bank shouts to him, "Young man, young man, the rapids are not far away, you'd better pull for the shore." "You attend to your own business; I will take care of myself," he replies. Like a great many people here, and ministers, too, they don't want any evangelist here—don't want any help, however great the danger ahead. On he goes, sitting coolly in his boat. Now he has got a little nearer, and a man from the bank of the river sees his danger, and shouts, "Stranger, you'd better pull for the shore; if you go further you'll be lost. You can be saved now if you pull in." "Mind your business, and you'll have enough to do; I'll take care of myself." Like a good many men, he is asleep to the danger that's hanging over him while he is in the current. And I say, drinking young man, don't you think you are standing still. You are in the current, and if you don't pull for a rock of safety you will go over the precipice.

On he goes. I can see him in the boat laughing at the danger. A man on the bank is looking at him, and he lifts up his voice and cries, "Stranger, stranger, pull for the shore; if you don't you will lose your life"; and the young man laughs at him—mocks him. That is the way with hundreds in Chicago. If you go to them and point out their danger, they will jest and joke at you.

By-and-by he says, "I think I hear the rapids—yes, I hear them roar"; and he seizes his oars and pulls with all his strength, but the current is too great, and nearer and nearer he is drawn on to that abyss, until he gives one unearthly scream, and over he goes. Ah, my friends, this is the case with hundreds in this city. They are in the current of riches, of pleasure, of drink, that will take them to the whirlpool. Satan has got them blindfolded, and they are on their road to the bottomless pit.

We hear some men say in a jesting way, "Oh, we are sowing our wild oats; we will get over this by-and-by." I have seen men reap their wild oats. It's all well enough sowing, but when it comes to the reaping it's a different thing. I remember I went home one night and found all the people in alarm. They had seen a man come running down the street, and as he approached the house he gave an unearthly roar, and in terror they bolted the door. He came right up to my door and, instead of ringing the bell, just tried to push the door in. They asked him what he wanted, and he told them he wanted to see me. They said I was at the meeting, and away he ran, and they could hear him groan as he disappeared. I was coming along North Clark Street, and he shot past me like an arrow. But he had seen me, and [he] turned and seized me by the arm, saying eagerly, "Can I be saved tonight? The devil is coming to take me to hell at one o'clock tonight." "My friend, you are mistaken." [I] thought the man was sick. But he persisted that the devil had come and laid his hand upon him and told him that he might have till one o'clock, and he said, "Won't you go up to my room and sit with me?" I got some men up to his room to see to him. At one o'clock the devils came into that room, and all the men in that room could not hold him. He was reaping what he had sown. When the Angel of Death came and laid his cold hand on him, oh, how he cried for mercy—how he beseeched for pardon.

Ah, yes, young men, you may say in a laughing and jesting way, you are sowing your wild oats, but the reaping time is coming. May God show you tonight what folly it is—what a miserable life you are leading. May we lift our hearts here to the God of all grace, so that we may see our lost and ruined condition if we do not come to Him. Christ stands ready and willing to save—to save tonight all those who are willing to be saved.

The Bible is filled with the call for people to repent and come to God in one form or another. Moody never failed in any sermon to make the same call. No matter what the message dealt with, he always encouraged the unconverted to renounce whatever it was holding them back and accept Christ.

Repentance is more than a feeling of sorrow for sin. It consists of totally turning away from the sin or sins that are preventing a person from coming to Christ. God hates sin and demands full repentance from the sinner.

Men such as Cain, Judas, and King Saul displayed signs of sorrow for their actions, but they never gave any evidence of totally turning away from their sin.

CHAPTER NINE

Repentance

You will find my text tonight in the seventeenth chapter of Acts, part of the thirtieth verse: "but now commandeth all men everywhere to repent." I have heard a number of complaints about the preaching here in the tabernacle, that repentance has not been touched upon. The fact is, that I have never had very great success in preaching upon repentance. When I have preached it people haven't repented. I've had far more success when I've preached Christ's goodness. But tonight I will preach about repentance, so you will have no more cause of complaint. I believe in repentance just as much as I believe in the Word of God.

When John the Baptist came to preach to the Jewish nation his one cry was, "Repent! Repent!" But when Christ came he changed it to, "The blood of the Lamb taketh away the sin of the world." I would rather cry, "The blood of the Lamb taketh away the sin of the world," than talk about repentance. And when Christ came [He said,] "Repent ye," but He soon pointed them to something higher—He told them about the goodness of God. It is the goodness of God that produces repentance.

When, upon the Day of Pentecost they asked what to do to be saved, [He told] men, "Repent, every one of you." When Christ sent His disciples out to preach, two by two, we find the message He gave them to deliver was, "Repent ye, for the kingdom of heaven is at hand." It is clearly preached throughout the Scriptures. There is a good deal of trouble among people about what repentance really is. If you ask people what it is, they will tell you, "It is feeling sorry." If you ask a man if he repents, he will tell you, "Oh, yes; I generally feel sorry for my sins." That is not repentance. It is something more than feeling sorry. Repentance is turning right about and forsaking sin. I wanted to speak on Sunday about that verse in Isaiah, which says, "Let the guilty forsake his way, and the unrighteous man his thoughts." That is what it is. If a man doesn't turn from his sin he won't be accepted of God, and if righteousness doesn't produce a turning about—a turning from bad to good—it isn't true righteousness.

Unconverted people have got an idea that God is their enemy. Now, let me impress this, and I told you the same the other night, God hates sin with a perfect hatred; He will punish sin wherever He finds it. Yet He at the same time loves the sinner and wants him to repent and turn to Him. If men will only turn they will find mercy, and find it just the moment they turn to Him. You will find men sorry for their misdeeds. Cain, no doubt, was sorry, but that was not true repentance. There is no cry recorded in the Scriptures as coming from him, "O my God, O my God, forgive me." There was no repentance in him, only feeling sorry. Look at Judas. There is no sign that he turned to God—no sign that he came to Christ asking forgiveness. Yet he probably felt sorry. He was very likely filled with remorse and despair; but he didn't repent. Repentance is turning to Him who loved us and gave Himself for us. Look at King Saul, and see the difference between him and King David. David fell as low as Saul and a good deal lower—he fell from a higher pinnacle—but what was the difference between the two? David turned back to God and confessed his sin and was forgiven. But look at King Saul. There was no repentance there, and God couldn't save him till he repented.

You will find, all through the Scriptures, where men have repented God has forgiven them. Look at that publican when he went up to pray; he felt his sin so great that he couldn't look up to heaven—all he could do was to smite his heart and cry, "God forgive me a sinner." There was turning to God—repentance—and that man went down to his home forgiven. Look at that prodigal. His father couldn't forgive him while he was still in a foreign land and squandering his money in riotous living, but the moment he came home repentant, how soon that father forgave him—how quickly he came to meet him with the word of forgiveness. It wouldn't have done any good to forgive the boy while he was in that foreign country unrepentant. He would have despised all favors and blessings from his father. That is the position [in which] the sinner stands toward God. He cannot be forgiven and get His blessing until he comes to God repenting of all his sins and asking the blessing.

Now, we read in Scripture that God deals with us as a father deals with a son. Fathers and mothers, you who have children, let me ask by way of illustration, suppose you go home, and you find that while you have been here your boy has gone to your private drawer and stolen five dollars of your money. You go to him and say, "John, did you take that money?" "Yes, father, I took that money," he replies. When you hear him saying this without any apparent regret, you won't forgive him. You want to get at his conscience; you know it would do him an injury to forgive him unless he confesses his wrong. Suppose he won't do it. "Yes," he says, "I stole your money, but I don't think I've done wrong." The mother cannot, the father cannot forgive him, unless he sees he has done wrong, and wants forgiveness.

That's the trouble with the sinners in Chicago. They've turned against God, broken His commandments, trampled His law under their feet, and their sins hang upon them; until they show signs of repentance their sin will remain. But the moment they see their iniquity and come to God, forgiveness will be given them and their iniquity will be taken out of their way. Said a person to me the other day, "It is my sin that stands between me and Christ." "It isn't," I replied, "it's your own will." That's what stands between the sinner and forgiveness. Christ will take all your iniquities away if you will. Men are so proud that they won't acknowledge and confess before God. Don't you see on the face of it, if your boy won't repent you cannot forgive him, and how is God going to forgive a sinner if he doesn't repent? If He was allowing an unrepentant sinner into His kingdom, there would be war in heaven in twenty-four hours. You cannot live in a house with a boy who steals everything he can lay his hands on. You would have to banish him from your house.

Look at King David [and] his son Absalom. After he had been sent away he got his friends to intercede for him to get him back to Jerusalem. They succeeded in getting him back to the city, but someone told the king that he hadn't repented, and his father would not see him. After he had been in Jerusalem some time, trying his best to get into favor and position again without repentance, he sent a friend, Joab, to the king, and told him to say to his father, "Examine me, and if you find no iniquity in me, take me in." He was forgiven, but the most foolish thing King David ever did was to forgive that young prince. What was the result? He drove him from the throne. That's what the sinner would do if he got into heaven unrepentant. He would just drive God from the throne—tear the crown from Him. No unrepentant sinner can get into the kingdom of heaven.

Ah, some people say, "I believe in the mercy of God; I don't believe God will allow one to perish; I believe everyone will get to heaven." Look at those antediluvians. Do you think He swept all those sinners, all those men and women who were too wicked to live on earth—do you believe He swept them all into heaven and left the only righteous man to wade through the flood? Do you think He would do this? And yet many men believe all will go into heaven. The day will come when you will wake up and know that you have been deceived by the devil. No unrepentant sinner will ever get into heaven; unless he forsakes his sin he cannot enter there. The law of God is very plain on this point: "Except a man repent." That's the language of Scripture. And when this is so plainly set down, why is it that men fold their arms and say, "God will take me into heaven anyway."

Suppose a governor elected today comes into office in a few months, and he finds a great number of criminals in prison, and he goes and says, "I feel for those prisoners. They cannot stay in jail any longer." Suppose some murders have been committed, and he says, "I am tender hearted; I can't punish those men," and he opens the prison door and lets them all out. How long would that governor be in his position? These very men who are depending on the mercy of God would be the first to raise their voice against that governor. These men would say, "These murderers must be punished or society will be imperiled; life will not be safe." And yet they believe in the mercy of God whether they repent or not. My dear friends, don't go on under that delusion; it is a snare of the devil. I tell you the Word of God is true, and it tells us, "Except a man repent" there is not one ray of hope held out. May the Spirit of God open your eyes tonight and show you the truth—let it go into your hearts. "Let the wicked forsake his way and the unrighteous his thoughts."

Now, my friends, repentance is not fear. A great many people say I don't preach up the terrors of religion. I don't want to—don't want to scare men into the kingdom of God. I don't believe in preaching that way. If I did get some in that way they would soon get out. If I wanted to scare men into heaven I would just hold the terror of hell over their heads and say, "Go right in." But that's not the way to win men. They don't have any slaves in heaven. They are all sons, and they must accept salvation voluntarily. Terror never brought a man in yet.

Look at a vessel tossed upon the billows, and sailors think it is going to the bottom and death is upon them. They fall down on their knees. And you would think they were all converted. They are not converted; they're only scared. There's no repentance there, and as soon as the storm is over and they get on shore, they are the same as ever. All their terror has left them—they've forgotten it, and they fall into their old habits. How many men have, while lying on a sick bed, and they thought they saw the terrors of death gathering around them, made resolutions to live a new life if they only get well again? But the moment they get better they forget all about their resolutions. It was only fear with them; that's not what we want to feel. Fear is one thing, and repentance is another. True repentance is the Holy Ghost showing sinners their sin. That's what we want. May the Holy Ghost reveal to each one out of Christ here tonight their lost condition unless they repent.

If God threw Adam out of Eden on account of one sin, how can you expect to get into the heavenly paradise with ten thousand? I can imagine someone saying, "I haven't got anything to repent of." If you are one of those Pharisees, I can tell you that this sermon will not reach your heart. I would like to find one man who could come up here and say, "I have no sin." If I was one of those who thought I had no sin to repent of, I'd never go to church; I would certainly not come up to the tabernacle. But could you find a man walking the streets of Chicago who could say this honestly? I don't believe there's a day passed over my head during the last twenty years but when night came I found I had some sin to repent of.

It is impossible for a man to live without sinning. There are so many things to draw away the heart and affections of men from God. I feel as if I ought to be repenting all the time. Is there a man here who can say honestly, "I have not got a sin that I need ask forgiveness for"? "I haven't one thing to repent of"? Some men seem to think that God has got ten different laws for each of those Ten Commandments, but if you have been guilty of breaking one you are guilty of breaking all. If a man steals five dollars and another steals five hundred dollars, the one is as guilty of theft as the other. A man who has broken one commandment of God is as guilty as he who has broken ten. If a man doesn't feel this, and come to Him repentant and turn his face from sin toward God, there is not a ray of hope. Nowhere can you find one ray from Genesis to Revelation. Don't go out of this tabernacle saying, "I have nothing to repent."

I heard of a man who said he had been converted. A friend asked him if he had repented. "No," said he, "I never trouble my head about it." My friends, when a man becomes converted, the work has to be a little deeper than that. He has to become repentant, and try to atone for what he has done. If he is at war with anyone he has to go and be reconciled to his enemy. If he doesn't his conversion is the work of Satan. When a man turns to God he is made a new creature—a new man. His impulses all the time are guided by love. He loves his enemies and tries to repair all wrong he has done. This is a true sign of conversion. If this sign is not apparent, his conversion has never gotten from his head to his heart.

We must be born of the spirit; hearts must be regenerated—born again. When a man repents and turns to the God of heaven, then the work is deep and thorough. I hope that everyone here tonight will see the necessity of true repentance when they come to God for a blessing, and may the Spirit move you to ask it tonight.

I can imagine some of you saying, "How am I to repent tonight?" My friends, there are only two parties in the world. There has been a great political contest here today, and there have been two sides. We will not know before forty-eight hours which side has triumphed. There is great interest now to know which side has been the stronger. Now, there are two parties in this world—those for Christ and those against Him, and to change to Christ's party is only moving from the old party to the new. You know that the old party is bad, and the new one is good, and yet you don't change. Suppose I was called to New York tonight and went down to the Illinois Central Depot to catch the ten o'clock train. I go on the train, and a friend should see me and say, "You are on the wrong train for New York. You are on the Burlington train." "Oh, no," I say, "you are wrong; I asked someone, and he told me this was the right train." "Why," this friend replies, "I've been in Chicago for twenty years and know that you are on the wrong train," and the man talks, and at last convinces me, but I sit still, although I believe I am on the wrong train for New York, and I go on to Burlington. If you don't get off the wrong train and get on the right one, you will not reach heaven. If you have not repented, seize your baggage tonight and go to the other train.

If a man is not repentant his face is turned away from God, and the moment his face is turned toward God peace and joy follow. There are a great many people hunting after joy, after peace. Dear friends, if you want to find it tonight, just turn to God, and you will get it. You need not hunt for it any longer; only come and get it.

When I was a little boy I remember I tried to catch my shadow. I don't know if you were ever so foolish; but I remember running after it and trying to get ahead of it. I could not see why the shadow always kept ahead of me. Once I happened to be racing with my face to the sun, and I looked over my head and saw my shadow coming back of me, and it kept behind me all the way. It is the same with the Sun of Righteousness; peace and joy will go with you while you go with your face toward Him, and these people who are getting at the back of the Son are in the darkness all the time. Turn to the light of God, and the reflection will flash in your heart. Don't say that God will not forgive you. It is only your will which keeps His forgiveness from you.

My sister, I remember, told me her little boy said something naughty one morning, when his father said to him, "Sammy, go and ask your mother's forgiveness." "I won't," replied the child. "If you don't ask your mother's forgiveness I'll put you to bed." It was early in the morning—before he went to business, and the boy didn't think he would do it. He said, "I won't," again. They undressed him and put him to bed. The father came home at noon expecting to find his boy playing about the house. He didn't see him about, and asked his wife where he was. "In bed still." So he went up to the room, and sat down by the bed, and said, "Sammy, I want you to ask your mother's forgiveness." But the answer was, "No." The father coaxed and begged, but could not induce the child to ask forgiveness. The father went away, expecting certainly that when he came home at night the child would have got all over it. At night, however, when he got home he found the little fellow still in bed. He had lain there all day. He went to him and tried to get him to go to his mother, but it was no use. His mother went and was equally unsuccessful. That father and mother could not sleep any that night. They expected every moment to hear their little son knock at their door. Now, they wanted to forgive the boy. My sister told me it was just as if death had come into their home. She never passed through such a night. In the morning she went to him and said, "Now, Sammy, you are going to ask my forgiveness," but the boy turned his face to the wall and wouldn't speak. The father came home at noon, and the boy was as stubborn as ever. It looked as though the child was going to conquer. It was for the good of the boy that they didn't want to give him his own way. It is a great deal better for us to submit to God than to have our own way. Our own way will lead us to ruin; God's way leads to life everlasting. The father went off to his office, and that afternoon my sister went in to her son about four o'clock and began to reason with him. And, after talking for some time, she said, "Now, Sammy, say 'mother.'" "Mother," said the boy. "Now say 'for.'" "For." "Now just say 'give.'" And the boy repeated "give." "Me," said the mother. "Me," and the little fellow fairly leaped out of bed. "I have said it," he cried; "take me down to Papa, so that I can say it to him."

Oh, sinner, go to Him and ask His forgiveness. This is repentance. It is coming in with a broken heart and asking the King of heaven to forgive you. Don't say you can't. It is a lie. It is your stubborn will—it is your stubborn heart.

Now, let me say here tonight, you are in a position to be reconciled to God now. You are not in a position to deny this reconciliation a week, a day, an hour. God tells you, "Now."

Look at that beautiful steamer *Atlantic*. There she is in the bay, groping her way along a rocky coast. The captain doesn't know, as his vessel plows through that ocean, that in a few moments it will strike a rock and hundreds of those on board will perish in a watery grave. If he knew, in a minute he could strike a bell, and the steamer would be turned from that rock, and the people would be saved. The vessel has struck, but he knows now too late.

You have time now. In five minutes, for all you and I know, you may be in eternity. God hangs a mist over our eyes as to our summons. So *now* God calls—*now*, everyone repent, and all your sins will be taken from you. I have come in the name of the Master to ask you to turn to God now. May God help you to turn and live.

By the time Moody arrived on the evangelistic scene the biblical literacy rate in America had plummeted. There was a time in American history when more than ninety percent of the population read the Bible regularly. Sermons were full of illustrations taken directly from the Bible.

Unlike the other evangelists before and after him, Moody devoted several sermons to the topic of Bible study. According to him, the important tools for effective study are a large-print Bible, concordance, and a Bible dictionary.

Moody studied entire books, special biblical topics, as well as important Bible characters. Intensive Bible study contributed a lasting influence to his own life. He realized that a sermon would eventually be forgotten, but if his audience could be stimulated into the habitual study of God's Word, they would experience greater spiritual maturity.

CHAPTER TEN

How to Study the Bible

Part One

One thing I have noticed in studying the Word of God, and that is, when a man is filled with the Spirit, he deals largely with the Word of God; whereas, the man who is filled with his own ideas, refers rarely to the Word of God. He gets along without it, and you seldom see it mentioned in his discourses. A great many use it only as a textbook. They get their text from the Bible, and go on without any further allusion to it. They ignore it; but when a man is filled with the Word, as Stephen was, he cannot help speaking Scripture. You will find that Moses was constantly repeating the commandments. You will find too, that Joshua, when he came across Jordan with his people, there they stood, and the Law of the Lord God was read to them, and you will find all through Scripture the man of God dealing much with His Word. Why, you will find Christ constantly referring to them, and saying, "Thus saith the Scriptures." Now, as old Dr. Bonair of Glasgow said, "The Lord didn't tell Joshua how to use

173

a sword, but He told him how he should meditate on the Lord day and night, and then he would have good success."

When we find a man meditating on the words of God, my friends, that man is full of boldness and is successful. And the reason why we have so little success in our teaching is because we know so little of the Word of God. You must know it and have it in your heart. A great many have it in their head and not in their heart. If we have the Spirit of God in our heart, then we have something to work upon. He does not use us because He is not in us. Know, as we come to this word today, as Mr. Sankey has been singing:

> No word He hath spoken
> Was ever yet broken.

Let us take this thought in John 10:35: "and the Scripture cannot be broken." There is a great deal of infidelity around, and it has crept into many of the churches too. These doubters take up the Bible and wonder if they can believe it all—if it is true from [front] to back, and a good many things in it they believe are not true. I have a good deal of admiration for that black man who was approached by some infidel—some skeptical man who told him, "Why, the Bible is not true; all scientific men tell us that now; it's only a bundle of fables." "The Bible isn't true?" replied the black man; "Why, I was a blasphemer and a drinker, and that book just made me stop swearing, drinking, lying and blaspheming and you say it isn't true?'" My friends, the black man had the best of the argument. Do you think if the Bible was a bad book it would make men good? Do you think if it was a false book it would make men good? And so let us take our stand on the black man's platform and be convinced that it is true. When we take it into our hands, let us know that it is the Word of God and try to understand it. Many of the passages appear to us difficult to understand, but if we could understand it clearly from front to back at first, it would be as a human book, but the very fact that we cannot understand it all at once, is the highest proof that it is the Word of God.

Now, another thought is that a great many people read it, but they read it as a task. They say, "Well, I've read it through, I know all that's in it," and lay it aside. How many people prefer the morning paper in order to get news? They prefer it, but it is a false idea. This Bible is the only newspaper. It tells you all that has taken place for the last six thousand years, and it tells you all the news of the future. Why, seventeen hundred years before Christ, the people were told in it of the coming of Christ. They knew He was coming. The daily papers could not tell us of this. They may be written by learned men, brilliant editorial writers, but they couldn't have told this. If you want news, study the Bible—the blessed old Bible— and you will find it has all the news of the world.

Now we come to the question [of] how to study it. A great many read it as I used to read it, just to ease my conscience. I had a rule before I was converted to read two chapters a day. If I didn't do it before I retired, I used to jump out of bed and read them, but if you had asked me fifteen minutes after what I had read, I could not have told you. Now this is the trouble with many— they read with the head and not with the heart. A man may read his Bible, but when he has closed it you may ask him what chapter he read last, and he cannot tell you. He sometimes puts a mark in it to tell him; without the mark he doesn't know, his reading has been so careless. It is to keep him from reading it again. [That's] just as I used to do when hoeing corn. I used to put a stick in the furrow to mark the place where I had hoed last. A good many people are just like this. They pick up a chapter here, and there is no connection in their reading, and consequently [they] don't know anything about the Word of God. If we want to understand it we've got to study it—read it on our knees, asking the Holy Ghost to give us the understanding to see what the Word of God is, and if we go about it that way, and turn our face, as Joshua did, in prayer, and set ourselves to study these blessed and heavenly truths, the Lord will not disappoint us, and we will soon know our Bible. And when we know our Bible then it is that God can use us.

Let me say there are three books which every Christian ought to have, and, if you [don't] have them, go and buy them before you get your tea. The first is a good Bible—a good large-printed Bible. I don't like those little-printed ones which you can scarcely see—get one in large print. A good many object to a large Bible because they can't carry it in their pocket. Well, if you can't carry it in your pocket, [you can] carry it under your arm. It is showing what you are—it is showing your flag. Now a great many of you are coming in from the country to these meetings, and when you get on the cars, you see people who are not ashamed to sit down and play cards. I don't see why the children of God should be ashamed of carrying their Bibles under their arms in the cars. "Ah!" some say, "that is the spirit of a Pharisee." It would be the pharisaical spirit if you hadn't dipped down into heavenly truths, if you haven't the Spirit of God with you. Some say, "I haven't it." Suppose you don't read so many of these daily papers, and read the Bible a little more often. Some say, "I haven't time." Take time. I don't believe there is a businessman in Chicago who couldn't find an hour a day to read his Bible if he wanted to.

Get a good Bible, then a good concordance, and then a scriptural [dictionary]. Whenever you come to something in the Word of God that you don't know, hunt for its meaning in those books. Suppose after the meeting I am looking all over the platform and Dr. Kittredge says,

"What are you looking for?" and I answer, "Oh, nothing, nothing." He would leave. If he thought I hadn't dropped something he wouldn't stay. But, suppose I had lost a very valuable ring which some esteemed friend had given me, and I told him this. He would stay with me, and we would move this organ, and those chairs, and look all over, and by looking carefully, we would find it. If a man hunts for truths in the Word of God and reads it as if he was looking for nothing particular, he will get nothing.

When the men went to California in the gold excitement, they went to dig for gold, and they worked day and night with a terrible energy just to get gold. Now, my friends, if they wanted to get the pure gold they had to dig for it, and when I was there I was told that the best gold was [found] by digging deep for it. So the best truths are [found] by digging deep for them.

When I was in Boston I went into Mr. Prang's chromo establishment. I wanted to know how the work was done. He took me to a stone several feet square, where he took the first impression, but when he took the paper off the stone I could see no sign of a man's face; the paper was just tinged. I said I couldn't see any sign of a man's face there. "Wait a little," he said. He took me to another stone, but when the paper was lifted I couldn't see any impression yet. He took me up—up to eight, nine, ten stones—and then I could see just the faintest outlines of a man's face. He went on till he got up to about the twentieth stone, and I could see the impression of a face, but he said it was not very correct yet. Well, he went on until he got up, I think, to the twenty-eighth stone, and a perfect face appeared, and it looked as if all it had to do was to speak and it would be human. If you read a chapter of the Bible and don't see anything in it, read it a second time, and if you cannot see anything in it, read it a third time. Dig deep. Read it again and again, and even if you have to read it twenty-eight times, do so, and you will see the man Christ Jesus, for He is in every page of the Word. And if you take Christ out of the Old Testament you will take the key out of the Word.

Many men in the churches nowadays are saying that they believe the teachings in the New Testament are to be believed, but those in the Old are not. Those who say this don't know anything about the New. There is nothing in the Old Testament that God has not put His seal upon. "Why," some people say to me, "Moody, you don't believe in the Flood! All the scientific men tell us it is absurd." Let them tell us. Jesus tells us of it, and I would rather take the word of Jesus than that of any other one. I haven't got much respect for those men who dig down for stones with shovels in order to take away the Word of God. Men don't believe in the story of Sodom and Gomorrah, but we have it sealed in the New Testament: "As it was in the days of Sodom and Gomorrah." They don't believe in Lot's wife, but He says, "Remember Lot's wife."

So there is not a thing that men today mock at but the Son of God endorses. They don't believe in the swallowing of Jonah. They say it is impossible that a whale could swallow Jonah—its throat is too small. They forgot that the whale was prepared for Jonah; as one woman said, "Why, God could prepare a man to swallow a whale, let alone prepare a whale to swallow a man." We find that He endorses all the points in the Old Testament, from Genesis to Revelation. We have only one book—we haven't two. The moment a man begins to cut and slash away, it all goes. Some don't believe in the first five books. They would do well to look into the third chapter of John, where they will see the Samaritan woman at the well looking for the coming of Christ from the first five books of Moses. I tell you, my friends, if you look for Him you will find Him all through the Old Testament. You will find Him in Genesis—in every book in the Bible. Just turn to Luke 24:27, you will find Him, after He had risen again, speaking about the Old Testament prophets: "And beginning at Moses, and all the prophets, he expounded unto them in all the scriptures the things concerning Himself." Concerning Himself. Doesn't that settle the question? I tell you I am convinced in my mind that the Old Testament is as true as the New.

And He began at Moses and all the prophets.

Mark that, "all the prophets." Then in the forty-fourth verse:

And He said unto them, These are the words which I spake unto you, while I was yet with you, that all things must be fulfilled, which were written in the law of Moses, and in the prophets and in the psalms concerning Me. Then opened He their understanding that they might understand the scriptures.

If we take Christ out of the Old Testament what are you going to do with the psalms and prophets? The book is a sealed book if we take away the New from it. Christ unlocks the Old and Jesus the New. Philip, in teaching the people, found Christ in the fifty-third chapter of Isaiah, "All we like sheep have gone astray; we have turned every one to his own way; and the LORD hath laid on him the iniquity of us all." Why, the early Christians had nothing but the Old Testament to preach the gospel from—at Pentecost they had nothing else. So if there is any man or woman in this assembly who believes in the New Testament, and not in the Old, dear friends, you are deluded by Satan, because if you read the Word of God you will find Him spoken of throughout both books. I notice if a man goes to cut up the Bible and comes to you with one truth and says, "I don't believe this, and I don't believe that," I notice when he begins to doubt portions of the Word of God, he soon doubts it all.

Now the question is how to study the Bible. Of course, I cannot tell you how you are to study it; but I can tell you how I have studied it, and that may help you. I have found it a good plan to take up one book at a time. It is a good deal better to study one book at a time than to run through the Bible. If we study one book and get its key, it will, perhaps, open up others. Take up the book of Genesis, and you will find eight beginnings; or, in other words, you pick up the key of several books. The gospel was written that man might believe on Jesus Christ, and every chapter speaks of it. Now, take the book of Genesis; it says it is the book of beginnings. That is the key; then the book of Exodus—it is the book of redemption; that is the key word of the whole. Take up the book of Leviticus, and we find that it is the book of sacrifices. And so on through all the different books; you will find each one with a key.

Another thing: we must study it unbiased. A great many people believe certain things. They believe in certain creeds and doctrines, and they run through the book to get Scripture in accordance with them. If a man is a Calvinistic man, he wants to find something in accordance with his doctrine. But if we go to seek truth the Spirit of God will come. Don't seek it in the blue light of Presbyterianism, in the red light of Methodism, or in the light of Episcopalianism, but study it in the light of Calvary.

Another way to study it is not only to take one book at a time; but I have been wonderfully blessed by taking up one word at a time. Take up the word and go to your concordance and find out all about it. I remember I took up the word "love," and turned to the Scriptures and studied it, and got so that I felt I loved everybody. I got full of it. When I went on the street I felt as if I loved everybody I saw. It ran out of my fingers. Suppose you take up the subject of love and study it. You will get so full of it that all you have got to do is to open your lips and a flood of the love of God flows upon the meeting. If you go into a court you will find a lawyer pleading a case. He gets everything bearing upon one point, heaped up so as to carry his argument with all the force he can, in order to convince the jury. Now it seems to me a man should do the same in talking to an audience; just think that he has a jury before him, and he wants to convict a sinner. If it is love, get all you can upon the subject and talk love, love.

Take up the word "grace." I didn't know what Calvary was till I studied grace. I got so full of the wonderful grace that I had to speak. I had to run out and tell people about it. If you want to find out those heavenly truths take up the concordance, and heap up the evidence, and you cannot help but preach. Take heaven; there are people all the time wondering what it is and where it is. Take your concordance and see what the Word of God says it is. Let these men who are talking against blood look into the Word of God, and they will find if it doesn't teach that it teaches nothing else. When we preach about that, some people think we are taking our own views. But the Word says, "the life of all flesh is in the blood, and without blood there is no remission." The moment a man talks against blood he throws out the Bible. Take up Saul; study him. You will find hundreds of men in Chicago just like him. Take up Lot; study that character. Let me say right here that if we are going to have (and I firmly believe in my soul that we are going to have) a revival in the northwest—if we are going to have it, you must bring the people to the study of the Word of God. I have been out here for a good number of years, and I am tired and sick of these spasmodic meetings; tired of the bonfires which, after a little, are reduced to a bundle of shavings.

When I see men speaking to inquirers in the inquiry room without holding the Word of God up to them, I think their work will not be lasting. What we want to do is to get people to study the Word of God in order that the work may be thorough and lasting. I notice when a man is brought coolly and calmly and intelligently, that man will have a reason for being a Christian. We must do that. We must bring a man to the Word of God if we don't want this western country filled with backsliders. Let us pray that we will have a scriptural revival. And if we preach only the Word in our churches and in our Sunday schools, we will have a revival that will last to eternity.

Let us turn back to one of the Old Testament revivals, when the people had been brought up from Babylon. Look at the eighth chapter of Nehemiah:

> And Ezra the priest brought the law before the congregation both of men and women, and all that could hear with understanding, upon the first day of the seventh month. And he read therein before the street that was before the water gate from the morning until midday, before the men and the women, and those that could understand; and the ears of all the people were attentive unto the book of the law.

No preaching there; he merely read the Word of God— that is, God's Word—not man's. A great many of us prefer man's word to that of God. We are running after eloquent preachers—after men who can get up eloquent moral essays.

They leave out the Word of God. We want to get back to the Word of God. They had an all-day meeting there, something like this, "And Ezra opened the book in the sight of all the people; (for he was above all the people;) and when he opened it all the people stood up" (Neh. 8:5). I can see the great crowd standing up to listen to the prophet, just like young robins taking in what the old robins bring them,

> And Ezra blessed the LORD, the great God. And all the people answered, Amen, Amen, with lifting up their hands: and they bowed their heads, and worshiped the LORD with their

faces to the ground. . . . So they read in the book in the law of God distinctly, and gave the sense, and caused them to understand the reading *(Neh. 8:6, 8).*

Now, it strikes me it is about the height of preaching to get people that understand the reading of the Word. It would be a great deal better if a preacher would sometimes stop when he had a remark, and say, "Mr. Jones, do you understand that?" "No, I don't," and then the preacher might make it a little plainer, so that he could understand it. There would be a great difference in the preaching in some of the churches. He would talk a little less about metaphysics and science and speak about something else. "Then he said unto them, go your way, eat the fat, and drink the sweet, and send portions unto them for whom nothing is prepared: for this day is holy unto our LORD: neither be ye sorry; for the joy of the LORD is your strength" (Neh. 8:10). "For the joy of the Lord is your strength." If you will show me a Bible Christian living on the Word of God, I will show you a joyful man. He is mounting up all the time. He has got new truths that lift him up over every obstacle, and he mounts over difficulties higher and higher, like a man I once heard of who had a bag of gas fastened on either side, and if he just touched the ground with his foot, over a wall or a hedge he would go; and so these truths make us so light that we bound over every obstacle.

And when we have those truths our work will be successful. Just turn over to Jeremiah 20:9, to this blessed old prophet. There was a time when he was not going to speak about the Word of God anymore. Now, I just want to show you this, when a man is filled with the Word of God you cannot keep him still. If a man has got the Word, he must speak or die. "Then I said, I will not make mention of him, nor speak anymore in his name. But his word was in mine heart as a burning fire shut up in my bones, and I was weary with forbearing, and I could not stay." It set him on fire, and so a man filled with the Word of God is filled as with a burning fire, and it is so easy for a man to work when he is filled with the Word of God.

I heard of a man the other week who was going to preach against the blood. I was very anxious to see what he would say about it, and I got the paper next morning and I found there was nothing else there than scriptural quotations. I said that was the very best thing he could do. As we see in the twenty-third chapter of Jeremiah: "Is not my word like as a fire, saith the LORD; . . . that breaketh the rock in pieces?" Those hard, flinty rocks will be broken if we give them the Word of God. Those men in the northwest that we cannot reach by our own words, give them this, and see if they cannot be reached. Not only that, if we are full of Scripture ourselves give them what God says, you will find it easy to preach—you will say we haven't to get up so many sermons. It seems to me if we had more of the Word of God in our services and gave up more of our own thoughts, there would be a hundred times more converted than there are. A preacher, if he wants to give his people the Word, must have fed on the Word himself. A man must get water out of a well when there is water. He may dip his bucket in if it is empty, but he will get nothing.

I think the best thing I have heard in Chicago I heard the other day, and it has fastened itself upon my mind, and I must tell it to your ministers. We had for our subject in Farwell Hall the other day, the seventh chapter of John, when the Reverend Mr. Gibson said if a man was to come among a lot of thirsty men with an empty bucket they wouldn't come to him to drink. He said he believed that was the trouble with most of the ministers, as that had been the trouble with himself. He hadn't got a bucket of living water, and the people wouldn't come to him to drink. Just look at an audience of thirsty men, and you bring in a bucket of clear sparkling water, and see how they will go for it. If you go into your Sunday schools and the children look into your buckets and see them empty, there is nothing for them there. So, my friends, if we attempt to feed others we must first be fed ourselves.

There is another thing which has wonderfully helped me. That is to mark my Bible whenever I hear anything that strikes me. If a minister has been preaching to me a good sermon, I put his name down next to the text, and then it recalls what has been said, and I can show it to others. You know we laymen have the right to take what we hear to one another. If ministers saw people doing this they would preach a good deal better sermons. Not only that, but if we understood our Bibles better, the ministers would preach better. I think if people knew more about the Word than they do, so many of them would not be carried away with false doctrine.

There is no place I have ever been where people so thoroughly understand their Bibles as in Scotland. Why, little boys could quote Scripture and take me up on a text. They have the whole nation just educated, as it were, with the Word of God. Infidelity cannot come there. A man got up in Glasgow at a corner, and began to preach universal salvation. "Oh, sir," said an old woman, "that will never save the likes of me." She had heard enough preaching to know that it would never save her. If a man comes among them with any false doctrine, these Scotchmen instantly draw their Bibles on him. I had to keep my eyes open, and be careful what I said there. They knew their Bibles a good deal better than I did. And so if the preachers would get the people to read the Word of God more carefully and note what they heard, there would not be so much infidelity among us.

I want to tell you how I was blessed a few years ago, upon hearing a discourse upon the thirtieth chapter of Proverbs. The speaker said the children of God were like four things. The first thing was, "The ants are a people not strong," and he went on to compare the children of God to the ants. He said the people of God were like ants. They pay no attention to the things of the present, but go on steadily preparing for the future. The next thing he compared them to was the conies. "The conies are but a feeble folk." It is a very weak little thing. "Well," said I, "I wouldn't like to be as a coney." But he went on to say that it built upon a rock. The children of God were very weak, but they laid their foundation upon a rock. "Well," said I, "I will be like a coney, and build my hopes upon a rock." The Irishman said he trembled himself, but the rock upon which his house was built never did.

The next thing the speaker compared them to was a locust. I didn't think much of locusts, and I thought I wouldn't care about being like one. But he went on to read, they have "no king, yet they go forth all of them by bands." There were the Congregationalist, the Presbyterian, the Methodist bands going forth without a king; but by-and-by our King will come back again, and these bands will fly to Him. "Well, I will be like a locust; my King's away," I thought. The next comparison was a spider. I didn't like this at all; but he said if we went into a gilded palace filled with luxury, we might see a spider holding on to something, oblivious to all the luxury below. It was laying hold of the things above. "Well," said I, "I would like to be a spider." I heard this a good many years ago, and I just put the speaker's name to it, and it makes the sermon.

But take your Bibles and mark them. Don't think of wearing it out. It is a rare thing to find a man wearing his Bible out nowadays—and Bibles are cheap too. You are living in a land where there are plenty. Study them and mark them, and don't be afraid of wearing them. Now don't you see how much better it would be to study it? And if you are talking to a man instead of talking about your neighbors, just talk about the Bible, and when Christian men come together just compare notes, and ask one another, "What have you found new in the Word of God since I saw you last?" Some men come to me and ask me if I have picked up anything new, and I give them what I have, and they give me what they have. An Englishman asked me some time ago, "Do you know much about Job?" "Well, I know a little," I replied. "If you've got the key of Job you've got the key to the whole Bible," [he said.] "What!" I replied; "I thought it was a poetical book." "Well," said he, "I will just divide Job into seven headings. The first is the perfect man—untried—and that is Adam and Eve before they fell. The second heading is tried by adversity—Adam, after the fall. The third is the wisdom of the world—the three friends who came to try to help Job out of his difficulties. They had no power to help him at all. He could stand his scolding wife, but he couldn't stand them. The fourth heading takes the form of the Mediator, and in the fifth heading God speaks at last. He heard Him before by the ear, but he hears Him now by the soul, and he falls down flat upon his face. A good many men in Chicago are like Job. They think they are mighty good men, but directly they hear the voice of God they know they are sinners; they are in the dust. There isn't much talk about their goodness then. Here he was with his face down. Job learned his lesson. That was the sixth heading, and in these headings were the burdens of Adam's sin. The seventh heading was when God showed him His face. Well, I learned the key to the Bible. I cannot tell how this helped me. I told it to another man, and he asked me if I ever thought of how he got his property back and his sheep back. He gave Job double what he had, and gave him ten children besides, so that he should have ten in heaven besides his ten on earth.

Part Two

A great many are asking the question, will this work hold out? Are these young converts going to stand? Now

I am no prophet, nor the son of a prophet, but one thing I can predict that every one of these new converts that goes to studying his Bible and loves this book above every other book is sure to hold out. The world will have no charm for him; he will get the world under his feet, because in this book he will find something better than the world can give him. Now what I want to say to these young converts, and to old converts, is to love the Word of God. Set more and more store by it. Then the troubles in your Christian life will pass away like a morning cloud. You will feed and live on the Word of God, and it will become the joy of your soul.

Now, to help some of you to a right course in studying God's Word, I want to point out a number of texts that you might begin with, and then, in the same way, you can collect others. I want to call your attention first to a part of the fourth chapter of Matthew. A little boy in the seat there, while giving his experience the other day, felt so sure about his strength that he defied Satan. I trembled. Those of us who are older, and know more about the devil's power, know that we can only meet him with the Word of God. We can't withstand him by our feelings or by our being converted; he only laughs at such weapons.

Read in this fourth chapter, from the third verse on, and see how Christ overcame Satan. Not by His feelings, not because He had been baptized of John in Jordan, but by the Word of the living God. Three times Satan advanced to the charge, but every time he was thrust through by the sword of the Spirit. And that must be your sword. Don't say, like the little boy in Scotland, "Old Nick, just you get behind me," but say, "O Lord, just put him behind me." You can't do anything against Satan of yourself; you can only overcome him through Christ and by the Word of the living God.

Then take Romans 10:15 and 17. It shows there was a work done for you on Calvary, but that there is another work quite distinct from that. "And how shall they preach, except they be sent? . . . faith cometh by hearing, and hearing by the Word of God." How many mourning Christians there are who know little about God, and the reason is just that they do not study the Word of God. You are little acquainted with this precious book.

I don't see how Christians can habitually read the newspapers on Sunday. I wouldn't advise you even to read your religious weeklies on that day. I find too many are making these take the place of the Bible. Let us have one day exclusively to study and read the Word of God. If we can't take time during the week, we will have Sunday uninterrupted.

What can botanists tell you of the lily of the valley? You must study this book for that. What can geologists tell you of the Rock of Ages, or mere astronomers about the Bright Morning Star? In these pages we find all knowledge unto salvation; there we read of the ruin of man by nature, redemption by the blood, and regeneration by the Holy Ghost. These three things run all through and through them.

But let us stick to the thought: how to study this Bible. A favorite way with me is just to take up one word or expression and run through the different places where it is. Take the "I ams" of John; "I am the bread of life"; "I am the water of life"; "I am the way, the truth, and the life"; "I am the resurrection"; "I am all, and in all." God gives to his children a blank, and on it they can write whatever they most want, and He will fill the bill.

And then the promises. A Scotchman found 31 thousand distinct promises in the Word of God. There is not a despondent soul in this tabernacle this morning but God has a promise just to suit him. They abound even in the books of Job and Jonah.

And now let us follow on the thought, "What is God able to do?" Just get all the blessed texts on that subject to heart, and you can't help speaking for God. Then you can indeed say, "God is my Father, Jesus is my Savior, and heaven is my home." There is a blessed verse in the gospel of John. There is no more fruitful subject in the Bible than is opened up there. The conversions there and through the Bible, notice, are different from each other, though all resounding to the glory of God. Think of Nicodemus, the woman at the well, and Matthew the publican. And then the conversions in the Acts, and those of the Philippian jailer and Cornelius. We make a great deal more ado about this simple act than the Bible teaches. Conversion is just to believe on Christ and follow Him, and may be but the work of a moment.

Mr. Moody went on to say: Take up these texts of Peter having the word "precious"; "precious blood," "precious Christ," "precious faith," "precious trial of faith," "precious promises of God." Just take one word of the apostle, and trace it out.

Many persons do not believe in assurance as to salvation. Turn to the third chapter of the first epistle of John, "Beloved, now are we the sons of God, . . ." The fifth verse of that chapter says, "And ye know that he was manifested to take away our sins"; . . .and then we come to "I know that my Redeemer liveth." All the Bible puts it in that way. When it speaks of hope, it means a certain hope, not a doubtful hope. The "hope of a glorious resurrection" was a sure hope. Then the nineteenth verse, "And hereby we know that we are of the truth, . . ." and then, "We know that we have passed from death unto life . . ." and "Ye know that no murderer hath eternal life, . . ." and also, "Hereby we know that he abideth in us, by the spirit which he hath given us." (1 John 3:14, 15, 24) There is no reason, nay, there is no excuse, for Christians doubting that they are saved; it is presumptuous not to take God at His word. Again, the second verse of the third chapter of the epistle of John says, "Beloved, now are we the sons of God, and it doth not yet appear what we shall be; but we know that, when He shall appear, we shall be like Him; . . ."

190

So I find great comfort and advantage in just taking up the Word of God in this way and studying it with a view to some single truth. Take up in this way a single name or life or character. Thus Lazarus, in his different stages, is the type of the dead soul—the soul dead in trespasses and sins; then he is the saved soul; then the feasting, rejoicing soul; then he testifies to the goodness of God. Galatians shows how we are first called, then justified, then sanctified; all through there is a beautiful connection, and you have only to stand right with one of these thoughts and follow the trail out.

And then take up the Christian's growth in grace, Psalm twenty-three, verse two, "Lie down in green pastures;" "Sitting at the feet of Jesus"; Ephesians, chapter 6, verses 13 and 14, "He is able to make us stand"; Psalms, "Walk through the valley of the shadow of death;" Hebrews, chapter 12, verse 1, "Run with patience the race that is set before us"; Psalms 18, verse 21, and in Isaiah, chapter 40, verse 31, "They shall mount up with wings as eagles."

The Christian, these verses show, goes up higher and higher, like a balloon, till the world is lost to sight; till he becomes like Christ and possesses eyes that can gaze unblinded on the glory of the city of God.

Trust is an important part of life. But, according to Moody, the most *important act of trust is to depend on Christ for salvation. In this chapter, an onlooker gives his account of Moody's "inquiry room talk." The inquiry room was where men and women could discuss their spiritual condition with trained workers who, in turn, pointed the way to Christ.*

Moody compares trust in Christ with that of a boy's trust in a mother's promise or the leap of a child into the arms of her father. Likewise, God tells men and women to have simple, childlike trust in Him.

God never forsakes those who trust in Him, and He is always with His children just as the parent is there for his child.

CHAPTER ELEVEN

Trust

Mr. Moody said in opening his regular address he would make the sermon an inquiry room talk. He was not going to have anyone in the congregation go away and say they hadn't an offer of salvation. He was going to turn the tabernacle into an inquiry room. And first he would call attention to a verse in the Psalms. Some who had counted the verses in the Bible found that the eighth and ninth verses of the one hundred and eighteenth Psalm were the middle verses of the Bible: "It is better to trust in the LORD than to put confidence in man. It is better to trust in the LORD than to put confidence in princes." And also he read the third and fourth verses of the twenty-sixth chapter of Isaiah: "Thou wilt keep him in perfect peace, whose mind is stayed on thee: because he trusteth in thee. Trust ye in the LORD forever: for in the LORD JEHOVAH is everlasting strength."

A boy whose mother promises him anything knows how to trust her. If she promises him a pair of skates at Christmas, he doesn't begin to analyze what trust is; he doesn't begin to ask what his feeling is. He simply says,

"Mother said so, and that's enough." There was nothing miraculous about it; it was simply trust. This is the idea of trusting in God. They must trust God, even if they don't know what the result will be.

In the sixty-second Psalm, eighth verse it said, "Trust in him at all times; ye people, pour out your heart before him: God is a refuge for us. . . ." It was the same in the midnight darkness as in the daylight. It was the child in the light whose father was in the dark. The child leaped into [her] father's arms though [she] didn't see him. It was the simple trust that the father was there.

Trust God at all times. Trust Him as one would trust a banker whom he had tried, a doctor whom he had confidence in; or a lawyer who had been tried and had never lost a case. They had an advocate with the Father, even Jesus Christ the Righteous. How to trust Him was shown in Proverbs to be with "all the heart"; not a little but with the whole heart. Don't trust the minister with the soul's salvation, but [trust] God. God wants the whole heart; God hates half-heartedness; God detests half-heartedness.

An incident of Alexander's [reign] illustrated this, where the emperor was warned to beware of his medicine. The emperor took the note of warning in one hand and the medicine in the other, and, because he trusted in his physician, took his draft. That was perfect trust. Paul said, "I am persuaded that He is able to keep that which I have committed unto Him."

The next step was, Who will trust Him? This is answered in the ninth Psalm at the tenth verse: "And they that know thy name will put their trust in thee. . . ." He must be known to be trusted; He must be believed to be trusted. No infidel could trust God because he didn't know Him. No one could go down to hell trusting in God. Then came the trust: "Thou wilt keep them in perfect peace that trust thee."

In the sixteenth chapter of Proverbs, at the twentieth

verse, was described the joy of the one who trusted God: "whoso trusteth in the Lord, happy is he." In the thirty-second Psalm, at the tenth verse again it was said, "Many sorrows shall be to the wicked: but he that trusteth in the Lord, mercy shall compass him about." The joy is thus described in the fifth Psalm, at the eleventh verse: "But let all those that put their trust in thee rejoice: let them ever shout for joy, because thou defendest them: let them also that love thy name be joyful in thee."

The inquirer asked about feeling—how should he feel? He [Moody] would say, "Let your feelings take care of themselves, you have only to come to God." They couldn't be saved by their feelings, nor by their good morals—by trying to break off their sins here and there. It was like lopping off the twigs of a tree, while Christ laid the axe to the root. In the twenty-ninth chapter of Proverbs it was said, "Whoso putteth his trust in the Lord shall be safe," or in the margin, "set on high."

The next question was: Why didn't they get this trust? Was it pride; the fear of neighbors? Why didn't they get this trust? Again in the thirty-seventh Psalm reference was [made] to this: "Fret not thyself because of evildoers, . . . Commit thy way unto the Lord, and he shall bring it to pass." He was the widows' God, the orphans' God. Let none fret for the coming winter; the Lord will provide. He will be a present help. Mr. Moody told a number of illustrative incidents and was especially practical in urging all who feared for the winter to trust in God, to rest in Him, and He would never leave, never forsake them.

Conversion is often portrayed as a long process that consists of several stages before completion. In this selection Moody addresses the issue of sudden conversion.

Using many examples from the Bible, he shows that sudden conversion is not the abhorrent teaching that it was apparently said to be in his day. It merely consists of one realizing his or her lost condition and turning to God for salvation. No lengthy process is involved, and nothing beyond turning to God for help is required. Once a sinner realizes the need for salvation and acts on that realization, conversion takes place. No special feelings are necessary because feelings can deceive.

God desires everyone to come to Him, and whenever a person makes that decision in simple faith, God is faithful to save, with or without emotional "evidence." Conversions vary from person to person. What is important is that one has forsaken sin and accepted Christ.

CHAPTER TWELVE

Sudden Conversion

I propose tonight to take a subject rather than a text, and that subject is sudden conversion—instant salvation. One reason why I am led to take up this subject is because I have received a large number of letters asking me how it is that I can teach such a pernicious doctrine that a man can be saved all at once—that salvation is instantaneous. One of the writers goes on to state that it is clearly taught in the Word of God that conversion is a gradual thing—that it is a life work—and that it is a dangerous thing to teach that a man can come into this tabernacle a sinner and go out a saved man. Now, let us see what is taught in the Word of God, and if it doesn't teach instantaneous salvation, let us give up the idea. I hold to it as I do to my life, and I would as quickly give up my life as give up this doctrine, unless it can be proved that it is not according to the Word of God.

Now, I will admit that light is one thing and birth is another. A soul must be born before it can see light. A child must be born before it can be taught; it must be born before it can walk; it must be born before it can be educated. I think the grandest mistake among ministers is that they are talking to dead men; that they are talking to men in the flesh instead of men born of God. Now, let us get them into Christ, and then educate them and build them up to the highest faith. Let us not try to teach men who are not born of God. The Scripture is very clear on this point. It gives no uncertain sound. If a man is dead in sin you may as well talk to a corpse as talk to him about spiritual things. To tell an unrenewed man—an unregenerated man to worship, serve, and love God, is absurd; you may as well tell a man to leap over Lake Michigan as to tell a man not born of God to serve Him.

Now the first illustration I want to call your attention to is when the voice came down from heaven to Noah: "Come thou and all thy home into the ark, for thee have I seen righteous before me in this generation." Now, there was a minute when Noah was outside the ark, and another when he was inside, and by being inside he was saved. As long as he was outside of the ark he was exposed to the wrath of God just like the rest of those antediluvians. If he stayed out, and remained with those antediluvians, he would have been swept away, as they were. It was not his righteousness, it was not his faith nor his works that saved him; it was the ark. And my friends, we have not, like Noah, to be one hundred and twenty years making an ark for our safety. God has provided an ark for us, and the question is: are you inside or outside this ark? If you are inside you are safe; if you are outside you are not safe. If you are outside you are exposed to the wrath of God continually, and you cannot tell the day nor the hour nor the minute when you may be swept into eternity.

When I was in Manchester in one of the inquiry meetings, I went up to the gallery to speak to some people there. While we were standing in a little group, a man came up and stood near us. He was a respectable-looking man, and I thought by his general appearance he was skeptical. I didn't think he had come up as an inquirer, but as I stood I noticed tears trickling down his face, and I went to him and asked him if he wanted to seek Christ, and he answered, "Yes." I went on talking to him, but he could not see what I meant. I thought I would use an illustration, and after I had put it to him I asked him if he saw it. He said, "No." I gave him another illustration, and asked him, "Do you see it now?" But he again replied, "No." I used two or three more illustrations, but he could not see them. He told me, "Mr. Moody, the fact is I do not feel the evidence of God." "But," I said, "I tell you you are not to be saved by your feelings," and I gave him this illustration; "What was it that saved Noah? Was it his ark, or was it his feelings, or his life, or his prayers?" "I see it now; it's all right," and he went away. This was Thursday night, and he had to leave on a night train. On the Sunday afternoon, while preaching in the Free Trade Hall, a man came and tapped me on the shoulder, and asked me if I knew him. I said, "No," and he said, "Do you remember when you spoke to me on Thursday and used the illustration of Noah's ark to save me?" "Yes," I answered. "Well, I got in then, and have been there ever since. The ark keeps me. Thank God for that illustration of the ark." May God help you to see this illustration tonight, and may you not be trying to save yourselves by your feelings, your tears, by your wounds. God has provided an ark, and every man who is in it is saved, and everyone who is out of it is lost.

Let us take another Bible illustration. Look at those two angels coming down to Sodom. They knew that God was going to destroy it utterly, and they led Lot out. What was it that saved his life? Was it his feelings, his tears? It was by obeying the call: "Escape for your life." And now God says, "Escape for your life"—escape to Mount Calvary. Don't delay, because He is going to destroy this world as He did Sodom. While Lot was in Sodom he was liable to the wrath of God, but the moment he got outside of Sodom he was safe. As long as a man remains out of Christ he is liable to the wrath of God and the fire of heaven. Look again, look at those children of Israel when they were commanded to put the blood on the doorposts and they would be saved from the hand of death. What was it that saved them? Was it the blood, or was it their feelings? The moment the blood was there they were saved; and if a man is behind the blood he is as safe as if he were walking the crystal pavement of heaven. When the blood was there the Angel of Death passed over. One moment the blood was off the posts, and the next moment it was on. It was instantaneous salvation.

You know Joshua received a command from God that he should erect six cities, three on each side of the Jordan, which were to be cities of refuge. There were to be great turnpikes and highways to these cities which were to be kept in proper repair, and the gates of the cities were to be kept open day and night, and signposts were to be placed along the road to provide for the man's guidance to these cities of refuge. The moment a man got inside one of those cities he was safe. His safety was instantaneous—the moment he stepped over the boundary line.

Just look at two men out in the woods chopping wood. As one of the men brings his ax down on the tree, it splits and flies from his hand and kills his companion. He knows what the consequences will be when the killing is discovered. He knows that it will be sure death the moment the news reaches the nearest relative of the deceased. The man who will not avenge the death of his relative is not considered a true man. If a relative would not avenge the death of a kinsman it was considered very dishonorable among the Israelites. The man knows that there is a city of refuge ten miles away, and if he can but reach it he is safe. Thank God, our city of refuge is not ten miles away. That man just leaps upon the highway. He does not take time to argue or think; he just leaps upon the highway and makes for the city of refuge. The news soon spreads that a man has been killed, and the murderer is making for the city of refuge. Whenever the brother learns that his kinsman has been killed, he starts after that poor fugitive. On they go—the avenger and the fugitive flying to his haven of hope. It is a life and death struggle. Look at him! See him as he leaps ditches and speeds along the road. Some people see him flying past. "Make haste," they cry, "because the avenger is upon you. Fly for your life." Ah, sinner, you do not know how far the avenger is behind you. Tonight he may be upon you. We do not know the day, the hour, when he will overtake us. The avenger, he knows, now is after him. On he goes, bounding over every obstacle, his speed at its utmost, and his face resolutely set toward the gate wherein his safety lies. He is terribly in earnest. See him leap over the highway; see his bruises; and on he goes panting and nearly exhausted. He sees the gates of the city. The officers see him from the walls, and they shout, "Hasten on, for the avenger is drawing near! He is behind thee." One moment he is outside the walls—the next moment he is inside. He is a saved man. One moment out, the next moment in. What are these illustrations in the Bible for unless to show us how we are to be saved? Don't you see from this that conversion is instantaneous? One minute you may be outside, and the next minute you are inside.

I will give you another illustration, which I think you will be able to get hold of. You will remember when we had slavery we used to have men come up from Kentucky, Tennessee, and other slave states in order to escape from slavery. I hope if there are any southern people here they will not think in this allusion I am trying to wound their feelings. We all remember when these black men came here how they used to be afraid lest someone should come and take them back. Why, I remember in the store we had a poor fugitive, and he used to be quaking all the time. Sometimes a customer would come in, and he would be uneasy all the time. He was afraid it was someone to take him back to slavery. But somebody tells him if he was in Canada he would be perfectly safe, and he says, "If I could only get into Canada, if I could only get under the Union Jack, I would be free." There are no slaves under the Union Jack he has been told—that is the flag of freedom, the moment he gets under it he is a free man. So he starts. We'll say there are no railways, and the poor fellow has got ten miles ahead when his master comes up, and he hears that his slave has fled for Canada and sets off in pursuit. Someone tells the poor fugitive that his master is after him. What does the poor fugitive do? What does he do? He redoubles his exertions and presses on, on, on, on. He was born a slave, and he knows a slave belongs to his master. Faster he goes. He knows his master is after him, and he will be taken if he comes up with him before he reaches the line. He says, "If I can only hold out and get under the English flag, the English government will protect me. The whole English army will come to protect me if need be." On he presses. He is now nearing the boundary line. One minute he is a slave and in an instant he is a free man.

My friends, don't mistake. These men can be saved tonight if they cross the line. Your old master, Satan, may be pressing down upon you, but there is a land of liberty up there, and the banner of heaven is that flag of love, and under the flag you are protected from all danger, and if an enemy comes near you God says, "If you touch him you touch the apple of my eye." And He will hold you in His right hand and keep you for the day of redemption. Will you go out of this hall tonight and doubt sudden conversion? Will you say a man cannot be saved all at once? Look what He said to Moses. He told Him to put a brazen serpent on a pole, and whenever a man looked at that serpent he would live. If some of the preachers we have now in Chicago had lived then they would have said a man may look six thousand years at that and he wouldn't be saved. A man would die while they were discussing it.

A few days ago, I heard of a minister who said I was preaching a most pernicious doctrine when I preached sudden conversion. But point out to me one single conversion in this blessed Bible that was not a sudden conversion. Why, every conversion recorded in the Bible was instantaneous, and if preachers tell men conversion is a life work they are keeping men out of the kingdom of God. We can have instant conversion. "Now is the day of salvation." I tell you sinners, escape for your lives, fly to the haven of safety—look, look, look, at the crucified One, and you will be saved tonight. Look and live. You will become a child of God for time and eternity. The blessing will come upon you—whenever we look we can be saved. Just go back to that camp of Israel. Everyone who looked at that brazen serpent was well. The remedy was instantaneous.

When I was in England they were at me all the time about this sudden conversion. They said it was a life work from the cradle down to the grave. I did all I could to show them it. One day I was walking down the streets of York when I saw a soldier coming down. You can tell a soldier in England in an instant by his coat. I stepped up to him and said, "My friend, I am a stranger in this country, and you will pardon me if I ask you a question. How long did it take you to become a soldier?" Well, he laughed in my face. I suppose he thought I was very green to ask him such a question. But he told me that he made up his mind to enlist in Queen Victoria's army, and he went to a recruiting sergeant, and he put an English shilling into the palm of his hand, and from that moment he was a soldier. When he had taken that shilling, from that moment he became one of the Queen's army, and if he goes back he becomes a deserter and, if caught, is put into prison. He first made up his mind to enlist, and that is the way to become a Christian. Make up your mind.

The next thing he did was to take the shilling, and from that moment he became a soldier. When you make up your mind to be a Christian, the next thing you have to do is to accept His terms—take salvation as a gift. You wonder how a man can become a Christian as that man became a soldier. He was a citizen one moment; the next moment he was a soldier. He was no longer his own master when he had accepted that shilling. He belonged to the English army. So the moment you enlist in Christ's army you belong to Him. If you want to become a Christian take Christ's shilling as a gift. The minute you take that gift, that minute you are a child of God. See what He says: To as many as receive Him gave He power to become the sons and daughters of [God]. When you accept Him He becomes your way, your truth, your light, your all in all. You can have His gift if you will receive Him tonight.

While I was in New York an Irishman stood up in a young converts' meeting and told how he had been saved. He said in his broken Irish brogue that I used an illustration and that that illustration saved him. And I declare that is the only man I ever knew who was converted without being spoken to. He said I used an illustration of a wrecked vessel, and said that all would perish unless some assistance came. Presently a lifeboat came alongside and the captain shouted, "Leap into the lifeboat—leap for your lives, or you will perish," and when I came to the point I said, "Leap into the lifeboat; Christ is your lifeboat," and he just leaped into the lifeboat of salvation and was saved. If a man goes out of the tabernacle tonight without salvation it won't be my fault; it will be his own. It will not be because the ark is not open, but because he will not accept the invitation to enter; it will not be because the blessing is not there, but because he will not take it, for it's there. May God open your eyes to accept Him before you leave this building—to accept salvation as a gift.

Moody was raised in a poverty-stricken, spiritually dead home. Because of his own difficult childhood he was fully aware of the importance parents play in the lives of their children.

His address to parents consists of stern warnings to be active in the conversion of their children. The home is the fundamental place for the gain or loss of a child's soul, and many parents have failed in bringing their children along the right path spiritually, only to experience sorrow in later years.

Both mothers and fathers are responsible for their child's spiritual development. Often fathers do not recognize the importance of their influence in such matters. If they display a disregard for religion, it is quite possible the sons will do the same. If a mother is too busy to nurture a religious desire in her child, she may find herself losing that child to sin. While the minister can only preach the gospel on a limited basis, the home can create a warm environment for its steady growth and eventual fruition in the life of a boy or girl.

CHAPTER THIRTEEN

Address to Parents

Part One

I want to call your attention to Deuteronomy 5:29. "Oh that there were such an heart in them, that they would fear me, and keep all my commandments always, that it might be well with them, and with their children forever!" And also the sixth chapter and seventh verse, "And thou shalt teach them diligently unto thy children, and shalt talk of them when thou sittest in thine house, and when thou walkest by the way, and when thou liest down, and when thou risest up."

I used to think when I was superintendent on the North Side, when I was laboring among the children and trying to get the parents interested to save their children, that if I ever did become a preacher I would have but one text and one sermon, and that should be addressed to parents, because when we get them interested their interest will be apparent in the children. We used to say, if we get the lambs in, the old sheep will follow, but I didn't find that to be the case. When we got the children interested in one Sunday, the parents would be some-times pulling the other way all the week, and, before Sunday came again, the impression that had been made would be gone. And I came to the conclusion that, unless we could get the parents interested, or could get some kind Christian to look after those children, it would al-most be a sin to bring them to Christ. If there is no one to nurse them, to care for them, and just to water the seed, why they are liable to be drawn away and, when they grow up, to be far more difficult to reach.

I wish to say tonight that I am as strong as ever upon sudden conversion, and there are a great many minis-ters, a great many parents, who scoff and laugh when they hear of children who have been brought unto Christ at these meetings.

Now, in many of the churches the sermons go over their heads; they don't do the young any good; they don't understand the preaching, and if they are impressed here we ought not to discourage them. My friends, the best thing we can do is to bring them early to Christ. These earliest impressions never, never leave them, and I do not know why they should not grow up in the service of Christ. I contend that those who are converted early are the best Christians. Take the man who is converted at fifty. He has continually to fight against his old habits; but take a young man or a young girl, and they get a character to form and a whole long life to give to Christ. An old man unconverted got up in an inquiry meeting recently and said he thought we were very hard-hearted down in the tabernacle; we went right by when we saw some young person. He thought, as he was old, he might be snatched away before these young people; but with us it seemed as if Christ was of more importance to the young than the old. I confess truly that I have that feel-ing. If a young man is converted he perhaps has a long life of fifty years to devote to Christ, but an old man is not worth much. Of course, his soul is worth much, but he is not worth much for labor.

While down at a convention in Illinois an old man got up, past seventy years; he said he remembered but one thing about his father, and that one thing followed him all through life. He could not remember his death, he had no recollection of his funeral, but he recollected his father one winter night, taking a little chip, and with his pocket knife whittling out a cross, and with the tears in his eyes he held up that cross and told how God in His infinite love sent His Son down here to redeem us, how He had died on the cross for us. The story of the cross followed him through life; and I tell you if you teach these children truths they will follow them through life. We have got so much unbelief among us, like those disciples when they rebuked the people for bringing the children to Christ, but He said, "Suffer little children to come unto me, and forbid them not, for of such is the kingdom of heaven."

I heard of a Sunday school concert at which a little child of eight was going to recite. Her mother had taught her, and when the night came the little thing was trembling so she could hardly speak. She commenced, "Jesus said," and completely broke down. Again she tried it, "Jesus said, suffer," but she stopped once more. A third attempt was made by her: "Suffer little children—and don't anybody stop them, for He wants them all to come," and that is the truth. There is not a child who has parents in the tabernacle but He wants, and if you bring them in the arms of your faith, ask the Son of God to bless them, train them in the knowledge of God, and teach them as you walk your way, as you lie down at night, as you rise up in the morning, they will be blessed. But I can imagine some skeptic in yonder gallery saying, "That's well enough, but it's all talk. Why, I have known children of ministers and Christian people who have turned out worse than others." I've heard that all my life, but I tell you that is one of the devil's lies. I will admit I've heard of many Christian people having bad children, but they are not the worst children. That was tested once. A whole territory was taken in which fathers and mothers were Christians, and it was found that two-thirds of the children were members of churches, but they took a portion of [the] country where all the fathers and mothers were not Christians, and it was found that not one in twelve of the children attended churches. That was the proportion.

Look at a good man who has a bad son. Do you want to know the reason? In the first place children do not inherit grace. Because fathers and mothers are good that is no reason why their children should be good. Children are not born good. Men may talk of natural goodness, but I don't find it. Goodness must come down from the Father of Light. To have a good nature a man must be born of God. There is another reason—a father may be a very good man, but the mother may be pulling in another way. She may be ambitious, and may want her children to occupy a high worldly position. She has some high ambition and trains the child for the world. Again, it may be the reverse—a holy, pious mother and a worldly father, and it is pretty hard when father and mother do not pull together. Another reason is, and you will excuse me the expression, but a great many people have got very little sense about bringing up children. Now, I've known mothers who punish their children by making them read the Bible. Do not be guilty of such a thing. If you want children not to hate the Bible, do not punish them by making them read it. It is the most attractive book in the world. But that is the way to spoil its attractiveness, and make them hate it with a perfect hate. There is another reason. A great many people are engaged in looking after other people's children and neglecting their own. No father or mother has a right to do this, whatever may be the position they hold in the world. The father may be a statesman or a great businessman, but he is responsible for his children. If they do not look after their children they will have to answer for it someday. There will be a blight in their paths, and their last days will be very bitter.

There are a great many reasons which I might bring forward if I had time; why good people's children turn out bad; but let me say one word about bringing up these children, how to train them in Christian ways. The Word is very plain: "teach them diligently." In the street cars, as we go about our business night and morning, talk of Christ and heavenly things. It seems to me as if these things were the last things many of us think about and as if Christ was banished from our homes. A great many people have a good name as Christians. They talk about ministers and Sunday schools, and [they] will come down and give a dinner to the bootblacks and seem to be strong patrons of the cause of Christ, but when it comes to talking to children personally about Christ, that is another thing. The Word is very plain: "teach them diligently." And if we want them to grow up a blessing to the church of God and to the world, we must teach them.

I can imagine some of you saying, "It may be very well for Mr. Moody to lay down theories, but there are a great many difficulties in the way." I heard of a minister who said he had the grandest theory upon the bringing up of children. God gave him seven children, and he found that his theory was all wrong. They were all differently constituted. I will admit that this is one difficulty; but if our heart is set upon this one thing—to have our children in glory—God will give us all the light we need. He is not going to leave us in darkness. If that is not the aim of your heart, make it this very night. I would rather, if I went tonight, leave my children in the hope of Christ than leave them millions of [dollars]. It seems to me as if we were too ambitious to have them make a name, instead of to train them up for the life they are to lead forever. And another thing about [discipline]: never teach them revenge. If a baby falls down on the floor, don't give it a book with which to strike the floor. They have enough of revenge in them without being taught it. Then, don't teach them to lie. You don't like that; but how many parents have told their children to go to the door, when they did not want to see a visitor, and say, "Mother is not in." That is a lie. Children are very keen to detect. They very soon see those lies, and this lays the foundation for a good deal of trouble afterward. "Ah," some of you say, "I never do this." Well, suppose some person comes in that you don't want to see. You give them a welcome, and when he goes you entreat him to stay, but the moment he is out of the door you say, "What a bore!" The children wonder at first, but they very soon begin to imitate the father and mother. Children are very good imitators.

A father and mother never ought to do a thing that they don't want their children to do. If you don't want them to smoke, don't you smoke; if you don't want them to chew, don't you chew; if you don't want them to play billiards, don't you play billiards; if you don't want them to drink, don't you drink, because children are grand imitators. A lady once told me she was in her pantry on one occasion, and she was surprised by the ringing of the bell. As she whirled round to see who it was, she broke a tumbler. Her little child was standing there, and she thought her mother was doing a very correct thing, and the moment the lady left the pantry, the child commenced to break all the tumblers she could get hold of. You may laugh, but children are very good imitators. If you don't want them to break the Sabbath day, keep it holy yourself; if you want them to go to church, go to church yourself. It is very often by imitation that they utter their first oath, that they tell their first lie, and then they grow upon them. And when they try to quit the habit, it has grown so strong upon them that they cannot do it. "Ah," some say, "we do not believe in children being converted. Let them grow up to manhood and womanhood, and then talk of converting them." They forget that in the meantime their characters are formed, and perhaps [they] have commenced to enter those dens of infamy, and when they have arrived at manhood and womanhood, we find it is too late to alter their character. How unfaithful we are. "Teach them diligently."

How many parents in this vast assembly know where their sons are? Their sons may be in the halls of vice. Where does your son spend his evenings? You don't care enough for him to ascertain what kind of company he keeps, what kind of books he reads; [you] don't care whether or not he is reading those miserable, trashy novels and getting false ideas of life. You don't know till it is too late. Oh, may God wake us up and teach us the responsibility devolving upon us in training our children.

While in London, an officer in the Indian army, hearing of us being over there, said, "Lord, now is the time for my son to be saved." He got a furlough and left India and came to London. When he came there for that purpose, of course God was not going to let him go away without the blessing. How many men are interested in their sons who would do as this man did? How many men are sufficiently interested in them to bring them here? How many parents stand in the way of the salvation of their children? I don't know anything that discouraged me more when I was superintendent on the North Side than when, after begging with parents to allow their children to come to Sunday school—and how few of them came—whenever spring arrived those parents would take their children from the school and lead them into those German gardens. And a great many are reaping the consequences. I remember one mother who heard that her boy was impressed at our meeting. She said her son was a good enough boy, and he didn't need to be converted. I pleaded with that mother, but all my pleading was of no account. I tried my influence with the boy; but while I was pulling one way she was pulling the other. Her influence prevailed. Naturally it would. Well, to make a long story short, some time after, I happened to be in the county jail, and I saw him there. "How did you come here?" I asked. "Does your mother know where you are?" "No, don't tell her; I came in under an assumed name, and I am going to Joliet for four years. Do not let my mother know of this," he pleaded. "She thinks I am in the army." I used to call on that mother, but I had promised her boy I would not tell her, and for four years she mourned over that boy. She thought he had died on the battlefield or in a southern hospital. What a blessing he might have been to that mother, if she had only helped us to bring him to Christ. But that mother is only a specimen of hundreds and thousands of parents in Chicago. If we would have more family altars in our homes and train [our children] to follow Christ, why, the Son of God would lead them into "green pastures," and instead of having sons who curse the mothers who gave them birth, they would bless their fathers and mothers.

In the Indiana Penitentiary I was told of a man who had come there under an assumed name. His mother heard where he was. She was too poor to ride there, and she footed it. Upon her arrival at the prison she at first did not recognize her son in his prison suit and short hair, but when she did see who it was, that mother threw her arms about that boy and said, "I am to blame for this; if I had only taught you to obey God and keep the Sabbath you would not have been here." How many mothers, if they were honest, could attribute the ruination of their children to the early training? God has said if we don't teach them those blessed commandments He will destroy us, and the law of God never changes. It does not only apply to those callous men who make no profession of religion, but to those who stand high in the church if they make the same mistake.

Look at that high priest Eli. He was a good man and a kind one, but one thing he neglected to do—to train his children for God. The Lord gave him warning, and at last destruction came upon his house. Look at that old man ninety-eight years old, with his white hair, like some of the men on the platform, sitting in the town of Shiloh waiting to hear the result of the battle. The people of Israel came into the town and took out the ark of God, and when it came into the camp a great shout went up to heaven, for they had the ark of their God among them. They thought they were going to succeed, but they had disobeyed God. When the battle came on they fought manfully, but no less than thirty thousand of the Israelites fell by the swords of their enemies, and a messenger came running from the field through the streets of Shiloh to where Eli was, crying, "Israel is defeated, the ark is taken, and Hophni and Phinehas have been slain in battle." And when the old priest heard it [he] fell backward by the side of the gate, and his neck broke, and he died. Oh, what a sad ending to that man, and when his daughter-in-law heard the news there was another death in that family recorded. In that house destruction was complete.

My friends, God is true, and if we do not obey Him in this respect He will punish us. It is only a question of time. Look at King David. See him waiting for the tidings of the battle. He had been driven from his throne by his own son whom he loved, but when the news came that he was slain, see how he cried, "Oh, my son Absalom, would to God I had died for thee." It was worse than death to him, but God had to punish him because he did not train his son to love the Lord.

My friends, if He punished Eli and David He will punish you and me. May God forgive us for the past, and may we commence a new record tonight. My friends, if you have not a family altar erect one tonight. Let us labor that our children may be brought to glory. Don't say children are too young. Mothers and fathers, if you hear your children have been impressed with religion, don't stand in the way of their conversion, but encourage them all you can.

While I was attending a meeting in a certain city some time ago, a lady came to me and said, "I want you to go home with me; I have something to say to you." When we reached her home, there were some friends there. After they had retired, she put her arms on the table, and tears began to come into her eyes, but with an effort she repressed her emotion. After a struggle she went on to say that she was going to tell me something which she had never told any other living person. I should not tell it now, but she has gone to another world. She said she had a son in Chicago, and she was very anxious about him. When he was young he got interested in religion at the rooms of the Young Men's Christian Association. He used to go out in the street and circulate tracts. He was her only son, and she was very ambitious he should make a name in the world, and wanted to get him into the very highest circles. Oh what a mistake people make about these highest circles. Society is false. It is a sham. She was deceived like a good many more votaries of fashion and hunters after wealth at the present time. She thought it was beneath her son to go down and associate with these young men who hadn't much money. She tried to get him away from them, but they had more influence than she had, and finally, to break his whole association, she packed him off to a boarding school. He went soon to Yale College, and she supposed he got into one of those miserable secret societies there that have ruined so many young men, and the next thing she heard was that the boy had gone astray.

She began to write letters urging him to come into the kingdom of God, but she heard that he tore up the letters without reading them. She went to him to try and regain whatever influence she possessed over him, but her efforts were useless, and she came home with a broken heart. He left New Haven, and for two years they heard nothing of him. At last they heard he was in Chicago, and his father found him and gave him thirty thousand dollars to start in business. They thought it would change him, but it didn't. They asked me when I went back to Chicago to try and use my influence with him. I got a friend to invite him to his house one night, where I intended to meet him, but he heard I was to be there and did not come near. Like a good many other young men, who seem to be afraid of me, I tried many times to reach him but could not. While I was traveling one day on the New Haven railroad, I bought a New York paper, and in it I saw a dispatch saying he had been drowned in Lake Michigan. His father came on to find his body, and, after considerable searching, he discovered it. All the clothes and his body were covered with sand. The body was taken home to that brokenhearted mother. She said, "If I thought he was in heaven I would have peace." Her disobedience of God's law came back upon her.

So, my friends, if you have a boy impressed with the gospel, help him to come to Christ. Bring him in the arms of your faith, and he will unite you closer to Him. Let us have faith in Him, and let us pray day and night that our children may be born of the Spirit.

Part Two

I have had a little trouble to find a text for tonight. All last night and this morning I was trying to find one but could not. This morning, however, in coming out of Farwell Hall prayer meeting, a mother whom I have known for a great many years came to me with tears running down her cheeks and nearly sinking to the floor with grief. "O! Mr. Moody," she said, "have these meet-ings to close and not one of my children saved?" and the thought flashed on my mind, "I have got a text." And it is in the ninth chapter of Mark, [verse nineteen] which we have read: "bring him unto me."

The disciples had failed to cure this man's son. James, John, and Peter had been with the Master upon the mount, where they had seen the transfiguration, and when they came down from that scene they found a great company around His disciples asking them questions. I suppose the skeptics were laughing and ridiculing the religion of Jesus Christ and its teachers. His disciples had failed—they had not been able to cast out the dumb spirit, and the father said, when asked a question, "I have brought my son to your disciples, and they cannot heal him." And He said, "bring him unto me." When he was brought, the devil threw him down. The moment the poor deaf and dumb man came into the presence of Christ, the spirit within began to tear at him. This is of-ten the case now. Sometimes when there is a good deal of prayer going up for people they become worse. When the Spirit begins with men, instead of getting better they sometimes become worse, and it seems as if God did not answer prayer; but this is only a sign that God is at work.

A mother was praying for and giving good counsel to a loved son lately, and he said [that] if ever she spoke to him about religion again he would leave the house. Whenever the Word was presented to him, he became worse. That mother did not take her son to the preachers, but thank God, she took him to Christ. She didn't take him to the church, she did not take him to her friends—she knew that if he was to be saved it was only by Jesus Christ. She took him to the Master, and the result was that within forty-eight hours after saying this to his mother, that wayward boy was brought to the feet of Jesus. So if any have been praying earnestly and faith-fully for their sons without success, my dear friends, get your eyes off the church, off friends, off everything else but Him, and let our prayer go up day and night, and it will be heard, because we have God's word [on] it. An answer is sure.

We are not sure whether the sun will rise tomorrow morning, but we are sure that He will answer our prayers. It is sure. If we hold on to God in prayer and find that we don't get our supplications answered in a month—in a year—we are to hold on till the blessing comes. Now, it may be that this mother, like a great many mothers, has been looking to the prayers here—looking to what has been going on in these meetings, and has been saying, "There are so many Christian people praying, and surely God will bless my boys owing to these prayers." Now, we must get our eyes off [of] multitudes, sermons, others' prayers, and let all our expectations be only from Him, and a blessing will come.

These meetings have been very profitable, and during the weeks past I have noticed that those fathers and mothers who have gone out after other people's children, have had their own wonderfully blessed. Whatever good you do to other people's children . . . will come back upon yours. It may be that that mother was very selfish, and wanted her sons blessed only; she hasn't, perhaps, been trying to bring others under the influence of the Lord Jesus Christ. Every day fathers and mothers come to me with tears in their eyes—fathers and mothers who have gone out after other people's children—testifying how their children have been blessed. A mother who has been working for Him here, told me that her five children—every one of them—had been blessed by these meetings, and I suppose that if I put it to the vote many parents here would stand up and testify as to the answers received to prayers and personal efforts for their children. I was very much surprised lately to see an old citizen coming into our meetings with a wayward son by his side night after night. Every evening he was to be seen with him, and last Monday evening he got up and told what God had done for him in answer to personal effort. That father woke up and did not rest till he was answered.

Now it seems to me, just as we are leaving this city, that a great many parents are beginning to wake up to the fact that these meetings are about to be closed, and their children have not been blessed. When we were in Great Britain, in Manchester, a father woke up to the fact that we were going away from that town. Just as we were about closing he got wonderfully interested in the meetings, and when we had gone to another town he said to his wife, "I have made a mistake: I should have taken you and the children and the servants to those meetings. Now I'm going to take my son from business, and take you and the children and the servants to the town where they are being held now and take a house and have you all attend the meetings." He came and took a house and sat down determined to remain there till all had been blessed. I remember him coming to me one night soon after arriving and saying, "Mr. Moody, my wife has [been] converted; thank God for that. If I get nothing else I am well paid." A few nights [later] he came in and said his son had become converted, and then told me one of the servants had been brought under the influence, and so he went on until the last day we were to be in that town arrived, and he came to me and said the last one of the family had yielded himself up to Christ, and he went back to his native city rejoicing. When we were in London the father and son came up and assisted in the work, and I don't know a happier man in all Europe than that one. How many parents living almost within sight of this building have felt no interest in these meetings; yet they know their children are hastening down to death and ruin. Business must be attended to [, and] time is very precious, and they have gone to waste, [as far as] bringing their sons and daughters under religious influences [is concerned]. And the result will be that many many a family in this city will see dark days and bitter hours, and many a parent will go down to their graves on account of wayward children. Now, why won't you even in the closing hours of these meetings—why won't parents wake up and bring their children to Christ? Just hold them up in the arms of [your] faith and pray, "Lord, Jesus, save these children that God has given me; grant, O God, that they may be with me in glory."

It may be that some father or mother is saying, "I have not been living right myself in God's sight; so how can I talk to my children of Him?" It seems to me the best thing to do under those circumstances is to make a confession. I knew a father who a few days ago told his children that he had not been living right. The tears rolled down his cheeks as he asked their forgiveness. "Why," said one child, "do you ask us for forgiveness? Why, father, you have always been kind to us." "I know I have, my child," he answered, "but I have not been doing my whole duty toward you: I've never had a family altar. I have paid more heed to your temporal welfare than to your spiritual, but I am going to have a family altar now." He took down his Bible and began there, and it wasn't long before his children were touched.

Suppose you haven't been living in accordance with the gospel: why not make an open confession to your wife—to your children—set up a family altar, and pray for your children? It will not be long before you will be blessed. Let us come to Him. Let us look straight away from the churches. Let us look from every influence to only the Master Himself, and let His words ring in the soul of every parent here tonight: "bring Him unto me." Have you got a wayward son? He may be in some distant state or foreign land, and by the last news you received of him was rushing headlong down to ruin. My friend, you can reach him—you can reach him by intercession at the throne.

A short time after I got here I received a letter from Scotland—I haven't time to read it. The letter was sent to a minister, and he forwarded it to me. It was the gushing of a loving father. He asked us to look out for his boy, whose name was Willie. That name touched my heart because it was the name of my own boy. I asked Mr. Sawyer to try and get on the track of that boy some weeks ago, but all his efforts were fruitless. But in Scotland that Christian father was holding that boy up to God in prayer, and last Friday, in yonder room, among those asking for prayer was that Willie, and he told me a story there that thrilled my heart. [He] testified how the prayers of that father and mother in that far-off land had been instrumental in affecting his salvation. Don't you think the heart of that father and mother will rejoice? He said he was rushing madly to destruction, but there was a power in those prayers that saved that boy. Don't you think, my friends, that God hears and answers prayers, and shall we not lift up our voices to Him in prayer that He will bless the children He has given us?

You know how Elisha was blessed by the Shunammite woman, and she was blessed in return by a child. You know how the child died, and how she resolved to go at once to the man of God. I can imagine Elisha sitting on Mount Carmel, and seeing that woman far off, and saying to his servant, "Do you see that woman? I think I know her face—it is the Shunammite, now that I see her face. Go run and ask her [if] it is well with her." Off the servant runs, and when the servant comes to her she says, "It is well." Although her child is dead she says, "It is well." She knows that the man who gave her the child could raise it up. She runs up to the master and falls down, putting her arms about his feet; and the servant tries to put her away. But Elisha won't let him. He says to the servant, "Here, take this staff and go and lay it upon the face of the dead child," and tells the servant to go home with her; but she won't leave the man of God.

She doesn't want to lean upon the staff or the servant. It wasn't the servant or the staff that she wanted, but the man of God that she wanted with her. "You come with me," she says. "You can raise him up." She would not leave him till he came to her house. He went in and closed the door and prayed to God that the child would be restored, and then lay upon the child, mouth to mouth, eyes to eyes, hands to hands, and the child began to sneeze, and there was the child of the Shunammite woman raised up. Bear in mind that it was not the servant nor the staff, but the Master Himself that saved the child. My friends, if we lean upon the Master we shall not be disappointed. The moment that child was brought to the Master the wish of that woman was granted, and if we as parents bring our children to Him, we shall not be disappointed.

But there is another thing I want to call your attention to. We don't fast enough. This fasting doesn't mean fasting from meat, as many people think necessary. It seems to me if I had a wayward boy I should put myself at the feet of Christ, and fast a little, by keeping away from amusements, [and] from theaters. I find a great many worldly Christians going off into the theaters. They say, "I only go for a little relaxation; of course, I could stop going whenever I like and needn't be influenced by them; I only go occasionally." A worldly Christian said to me, "I only go once a month." "Well," said I, "how about your boy; he may not have the will power you have, and your example in going only once a month may only be the means of his going there all the time." My friends, a man may have great will power, yet his son may have very little. Therefore, a little fasting in this regard would be good for our children.

We should abstain from all pleasures that are liable to be hurtful to our children. If you fathers and mothers want your children to keep from evil influences you ought to keep away from them yourselves. If they see you indulging in these pleasures, they think they are on the right side by doing the same thing. A young man says, "I don't want to be any better than my father; and he goes to the theaters." Now, there are young men who have come into the inquiry rooms one night and the next night have gone off to the theaters. I don't know if a man with the Spirit of God should go there. These men may one night be here and the next night may go off to some amusement where they hear as a waltz, "What Shall the Harvest Be" or "Almost Persuaded." How Christian men and women can go to such places as that, I cannot conceive. If it is not sacrilege, then nothing is. What can those worldly Christians expect from their children if they frequent such places? I think the time has come for a little fasting. When Christ died it was to separate His church from the world, and how can a man who has consecrated himself as a child of God, go back to the world without trampling that blood under his feet? When will the day come when a man of God shall make known by his conversation, by his actions, by his general appearance, that he has been freed from the curse of the world?

Then another thing. It seems to me that every man should have a family altar in his house. And if we cannot deliver prayers, let us take up each of our children by name; let us ask that Johnny, while playing with his schoolmates, may be kept from temptation. Why, we forget that a little child's temptations are just as much to him as ours are to us. The boy at school has just as heavy trials as we have. And then pray for Mary. If she is in trouble, bring it out and pray that God may give her power to overcome any besetting sin that she may have in her heart. I believe the day has come when we should have more religion in our families, more family altars. I believe that the want of this is doing more injury to the growth of our children than anything else. Why, long before the church was in a building, it was in the homes of the people. We can make the family altar a source of happiness. By it we can make the home the [most] pleasant place in the world. Let us, when we get up in the morning, bright and fresh, have some family devotions. If a man runs downtown immediately on getting up, doesn't get home until five o'clock, and then has family devotions, the children will be tired and [fall] sound asleep. And it seems to me that we should give a little more time to our children and call them around the altar in the morning. Or suppose we ask them to recite a verse, to recite a portion of a hymn—it must not necessarily be a long one—and, after that, have some singing, if the children can sing. Do not be in a hurry to get it out of the way, as if the service was a nuisance; take a little time. Let them sing some religious hymns. The singing need not be all psalms, but there should be a few simple religious hymns. Let the little children be free from all restraint. Then pray for each of them.

Another thing. It seems to me that we devote too little time to studying the Sunday school lesson. You know now we have a uniform lesson all over the country. That lesson should be taken up by parents and they should try to explain it to their children. But how many ever think of this—how many parents ever take the trouble to inquire even as to the kind of Sunday school teachers who instruct their children? And then we should take our children into the churches with us. It seems to me we are retrograding at the present day. A great many of our children are never seen in the churches at all. Even if the sermon doesn't touch them they are getting into good habits. And then if the minister says a weak thing, don't take it up, don't pick it out or speak of it before the children, because you are bringing your minister into disrespect with your children. If you have a minister whom you cannot respect, you ought to get out of that church as soon as you can.

Encourage them to bring the text home; let the Word be spoken to them at all times, in season and out of season. If the great Bible truths sink down into their hearts, the fruit will be precious: wisdom will blossom upon them, and they will become useful in the church and in the world. Now, how many parents will not take the trouble to explain to the children what the minister preaches? Take your children into the pews and let them hear the Word of God, and if they do not understand it show it to them. You know the meat they require is the same as we feed on; but if the pieces are too large for them we must cut it up for them—cut it finer. If the sermon is a hard one, cut it into thin slices so that they can take it. There was a time when our little boy did not like to go to church and would get up in the morning and say to his mother, "What day is tomorrow?" "Tuesday." "Next day?" "Wednesday." "Next day?" "Thursday," and so on till he came to the answer, "Sunday." "Dear me," he would moan. I said to his mother, "We cannot have our boy grow up to hate Sunday in that way; that will never do."

That is the way I used to feel when I was a boy. I used to look upon Sunday with a certain amount of dread. Very few kind words were associated with that day. I don't know that the minister ever said a kind thing or ever even put his hand on my head. I don't know that the minister even noticed me, unless it was when I was asleep in the gallery, and he woke me up. This kind of thing won't do. We must make Sunday the most attractive day of the week; not a day to be dreaded but a day of pleasure. Well, the mother took the work up with this boy. Bless those mothers in their work with the children. Sometimes I feel as if I would rather be the mother of John Wesley or Martin Luther or John Knox than have all the glories in the world. Those mothers who are faithful with the children God has given them will not go unrewarded. My wife went to work and took those Bible stories and put those blessed truths in a light that the child could comprehend, and soon the [boy's] feeling of dread for the Sabbath was the other way. "What day's tomorrow?" he would ask. "Sunday." "I am glad." And if we make these Bible truths interesting—break them up in some shape so that these children can get at them, then they will begin to enjoy them.

Now, there's no influence like a mother's, and if the mothers will give a little time to the children in this way, and read them some Bible story, or tell it [to them] in a simple way, it will not be long before the children know the Bible from beginning to end. I know a little boy, eleven years of age, who got up last Monday in the meeting and told how he found Christ. His father began by telling him Bible stories, and now he knows them as well as I do. The little fellow of eleven years is quite a preacher. Let us pick out the stories that will interest them from Genesis to Revelation, and that is the way to bring our children to Christ. It will fill them with the gospel—fill them with Christ. They will soon be so full of Jesus that when an infidel comes to unseat their faith, he will find no room for infidelity.

Now, New Year's Day is coming on. I haven't much time to speak about that now, but let me ask what are you going to do when the young men come to your homes on that day? Are you going to set wine before them? Are you going to tempt the sons of others to go astray? Don't offer them, I implore you, that hellish cup; don't be the instruments to lead the children of others away from the God of their fathers. I hope that in this city this infernal custom will soon be swept away. The idea of having some of our best young men reeling on the streets beastly drunk on the first day of the year is revolting, and yet there are Christians who, when young men visit them on New Year's Day, just urge the cup on them—press them to take it. They have got some new kind of wine, and they want them to taste it, and urge the young man just to take a little and the young man hasn't got will—hasn't got backbone enough to resist the temptation; [he] hasn't the power to say no. He goes to another house, and the same thing is repeated, and so on, until at night the poor fellow goes home intoxicated and breaks the heart of [his] mother. Remember when you offer the cup, if it is not to your own boy it is to somebody else's boy.

I have a great respect for that old woman who, with ribbons flying, ran into a crowded thoroughfare and rescued a child from under a wagon. Someone asked her, "Is he your child?" "No," she replied, "but he is someone's child." She had a mother's heart, and bear in mind when a young man comes to you, as you put the cup before him—remember, he is some other one's child. God has given us a charge, not only in looking to the salvation of our own children, but we have to see to the salvation of the children of others.

Now, let me say a word to the unfaithful fathers. At the close of this meeting, if you have been unfaithful to the children God has given you, why not stay and then go home and make an honest confession to your children? If you have a boy who is a reckless young man—if he is a drunkard, ask yourselves, "Have I done all that I could; have I ever set before him the truth of Christ?"

Not long ago a young man went home late. He had been in the habit of going home late, and the father began to [believe] that he had gone astray. He told his wife to go to bed and dismissed the servants and said he would sit up till his son came home. The boy came home drunk, and the father in his anger gave him a push into the street and told him never to enter his house again, and [he] shut the door. He went into the parlor and sat down and began to think, "Well, I may be to blame for that boy's conduct, after all. I have never prayed with him; I have never warned him of the dangers of the world." And the result of his reflections was that he put on his overcoat and hat and started out to find his boy. The first policeman he met he asked eagerly, "Have you seen my boy?" "No." On he went till he met another. "Have you seen anything of my son?" He ran from one to another all that night, but not until the morning did he find him. He took him by the arm and led him home and kept him till he was sober. Then he said, "My dear boy, I want you to forgive me; I've never prayed for you; I've never lifted my heart to God for you; I've been the means of leading you astray, and I want your forgiveness." The boy was touched, and what was the result? Within twenty-four hours that son became a convert and gave up that cup. It may be that some father has had a wayward son. Go to God, and on your knees confess it. Let the voice of Jesus sink down in your heart tonight. "Bring him unto me." A father whom I have known for many years said to me this afternoon, with the tears trickling down his cheeks, "I want to tell you something that I have never told in public. Forty-three years ago, when I was five years old, I was sick with scarlet fever, and my mother knelt down and prayed to God if it was His will, that her boy might be spared. My father was a drinking man, and she also prayed that I might be kept safe from the cup. My mother died early, but my mother's prayer has followed me all those years, and I have never touched one drop of liquor." Last night a young man, the son of that man, got up and told his experiences. Yes, the mother's prayer for her little boy, five years old, was answered. That prayer was answered. Why shall we not lift up our hearts in prayer for our children? Let us plead day and night till God saves them— till he brings them into the ark of safety. May the God of Israel save our children.

I remember being in the camp and a man came to me and said, "Mr. Moody, when the Mexican war began I wanted to enlist. My mother, seeing I was resolved, said if I became a Christian I might go. She pleaded and prayed that I might become a Christian, but I wouldn't. I said when the war was over I would become a Christian, but not till then. All her pleading was in vain, and at last, when I was going away, she took out a watch and said, 'My son, your father left this to me when he died. Take it, and I want you to remember that every day at twelve o'clock your mother will be praying for you.' Then she gave me her Bible and marked out passages and put a few different references in the flyleaf. When I had been gone four months, I took the watch, and it was twelve o'clock, but I remembered that my mother at that hour was praying for me. Something prompted me to ask the officer to relieve me for a little, and I stepped behind a tree out on those plains of Mexico and cried to the God of my mother to save me." My friends, God saved him, and he went through the Mexican war. "And now," he said, "I have enlisted again to see if I can do any good for my Master's cause." And the old man was down among the soldiers there preaching Christ. My friends, let us believe that God answers prayer, and let us not cease our supplication till salvation comes to our children, and all our little ones are brought into the ark of safety.

The conversion of men is very important to Moody because men are the leaders in the kingdom of God. He does not discount the importance of women, but he believes that men are harder to win to Christ. They do not see the importance of religion and are indecisive about spiritual matters.

Moody calls for a decision to be made by the men of the city: either follow God or Baal. To him there is not a third way, and the time to decide is now. The kingdom of God is at hand; enter it today.

Excuses abound, but for Moody the primary problem is a lack of moral courage to come forward. He hammers away at this issue and demands that every indecisive man hearing his voice come forward for salvation. This sermon resulted in the conversion of two thousand men.

❧

CHAPTER FOURTEEN

Address to Young Men

I want to call your attention tonight to a text which you will find in the eighteenth chapter of First Kings, twenty-first verse: "And Elijah came unto all the people, and said, How long halt ye between two opinions? If the Lord be God, follow him: but if Baal, then follow him. And the people answered him not a word." We find in this portion of the Word of God that Elijah was calling the people of Israel back; he was calling them to a decision as to whether they were for God or Baal, and a great many were wavering, just halting between two opinions, like the people of Chicago at the present time.

During the last eight weeks a great deal has been said upon the subject of religion. Men have talked about it all over the city. A great many are talking; a great many are taking their stand for, and a great many against Him. Now, what will you do tonight? I will just divide this audience into two portions—one against and one for Him. It seems to me a practical question to ask an audience like this, "How long halt ye between two opinions? If the

Lord be God follow him, but if Baal, then follow him." A man who is undecided about any question of any magnitude never has any comfort; never has any peace. Not only that, but we don't like a man who cannot decide upon a question. I like men of decision and firmly believe that more men are lost by indecision than by anything else. Am I not talking to many men tonight who intend someday to settle this question? Probably everyone here intends to make heaven his home, but Satan is trying to get you to put off the settlement of the question till it will be too late. If he can only get men to put [it] off till tomorrow, which never comes, he has accomplished all he wants.

How many in this audience have promised some friend years ago that they would settle this question? Maybe you said you would do it when you came of age. That time has gone with some of you, and it has not been settled yet. Some have reached thirty, some forty, and others have reached fifty years; their eyes are growing dim, and they are hastening toward eternity, and this is not settled with them yet. Some of you have promised dying brothers that you would meet them in that world; some have promised dying wives that you would see them in that land of light; and again, others have given their word to dying children that you would meet them in heaven. Years have rolled away, and still you have not decided. You have kept putting it off week by week and year by year. My friends, why not decide tonight? "How long halt ye between two opinions?" If the Lord be God serve Him; if not, turn your back upon Him. It seems to me a question every man can settle if he will.

You like those grand old characters in the Bible who have made a decisive stand. Look at Moses! The turning point in his life was when he decided to give up the gilded court of Pharaoh and cast his lot with God's people. You will find that every man who has left a record in the Bible has been [a] man of decision. What made Dan-

iel so great? It was because he was a man of decision.
What saved the prodigal? It was not that he got into his
father's arms; it was not his coming home. The turning
point was when he decided the question: "I will arise
and go to my father." It was the decision of the young
man that saved him. Many a man has been lost because
of indecision. Look at Felix, look at Agrippa. Felix said,
"Go thy way for this time; when I have a convenient season I will call for thee." See what Agrippa said: "Almost
thou persuadest me to be a Christian." Look at Pilate—
all lost; lost because of his indecision. His mind was
thoroughly convinced that Jesus was the true Christ. He
said, "I find no fault in Him," but he hadn't the courage
to take his stand for Him.

Thousands have gone down to the caverns of death for
want of courage. My friends, let us look this question in
the face. If there is anything at all in the religion of
Christ, give everything for it. If there is nothing in it—if it
is a myth, if our mothers who have prayed over us have
been deceived, if the praying people of the last eighteen
hundred years have been deluded, let us find it out. The
quicker the better. If there is nothing in the religion of
Christ let us throw it over, and eat, drink, and be merry,
for time will soon be gone. If there is no devil to deceive
us, no hell to receive us—if Christianity is a sham, let us
come out like men and say so.

I hope to live to see the time when there will only be
two classes in this world—Christians and infidels—
those who take their stand bravely for Him, and those
who take their stand against Him. This idea of men
standing still and saying, "Well, I don't know, but I think
there must be something in it," is absurd. If there is anything in it there is everything in it. If the Bible of our
mothers is not true, let us burn it. Is there one in this
audience willing to say and do this? If it is a myth, why
spend so much money in publishing it? Why send out
millions of Bibles to the nations of the earth? Let us de-

stroy it if it is false, and all those institutions giving the gospel to the world. What is the use of all this waste of money? Are we mad, are we lunatics who have been deluded? Let us burn the book and send up a shout over its ashes: "There is no God; there is no hell; there is no heaven; there is no hereafter. When men die, they die like dogs in the street!"

But my friends, if it is true—if heaven, if a hereafter in the Bible is true, let us come out boldly, like men, for Christ. Let us take our stand and not be ashamed of the gospel of Jesus Christ. Why, it seems to me a question that ought to be settled in this nineteenth century easily enough, whether you are for or against Him. Why, if Baal be God, follow him; but if the Lord be God follow Him. If there is no truth in the religion of Jesus Christ, you may as well tear down all your churches, destroy your hospitals, your blind asylums. It's a waste of money to build them. Baalites don't build blind asylums, don't build hospitals or orphan asylums. If there hadn't been any Christians in the world, there would have been no charitable institutions. If it hadn't been for Christianity you would have had no praying mothers. Is it true that their prayers have exercised a pernicious influence? Is it true that a boy who had a praying father and mother, or a good teacher, is no better off than a boy who has been brought up amid blasphemy and infamy? Is it true? It must be either one way or the other. Did bad men write that Bible? Certainly not, or they wouldn't have consigned themselves to eternal perdition. The very fact that the Bible has lived and grown during these eighteen hundred years is a strong proof that it came from God. Men have tried to put it out of the world; they have tried to burn it out of the world, but they have failed. It has come down to us—down these eighteen hundred years amid persecution, and now we are in a land where it is open to all, and no man need be without one. What put it into the minds of those men to give money liberally to print and circulate this book? Bad men wouldn't do this. This is a question that, it seems to me, couldn't be decided tonight. If it is not good, then take your stand. If the Lord be God, follow Him, but if Baal be God, then follow him. Someone asked Alexander how he conquered the world, and he replied that he conquered it by not delaying. If you want to conquer the devil you must not delay—accept eternal life as a gift tonight.

Let us take the surroundings of this text. We are told that Elijah stood before Ahab and told him [that] because of the evil deeds of Israel and the king, no rain would come upon the land for three years and a half. After that Elijah went to the brook Cherith, where he was fed by the ravens, after which he went to Zarephath and there dwelt with a poor widow for months and months. Three years and a half rolled away, and not one drop of rain or dew had come from heaven. Probably when Elijah told the king there would be no rain, he laughed at him. The idea that he should have the key of heaven! He [scoffed at] the very idea at first. But after a little it became a very serious matter. The brooks began to dry up, the cattle could not get water, the crops failed the first year, the next year they were worse, the third year they were even a worse failure, and the people began to flee out of his kingdom to get food, and yet they did not call upon Elijah's God. They had four hundred and fifty prophets of Baal and four hundred prophets of the groves, and yet all their prayers did not bring rain. Why did they not ask God for rain? Baal was not an answerer of prayer. The devil never answers prayer. If prayer has ever been answered, it has been answered by the God of our fathers, by the God of our mothers.

After Elijah has been gone three and a half years he returns and meets Obadiah the governor of the king's house. Ahab [has said to Obadiah,] "You go down that way, and I'll go down this way and see if we can't discover water." They haven't been separated long when

Obadiah meets Elijah and asks him to come to the king. The prophet tells him to go and say to Ahab, "Elijah is here." But Obadiah doesn't want to leave him. "If I lose sight of you this time, when the king knows you have stepped through my lands it may cost me my life. Don't you know I've been a servant of the true God all the time, and I've had a hundred of the prophets of the Lord in a cave? If you don't come I will lose my life." Elijah tells him to go and bring Ahab, and instead of Elijah going to Ahab, Ahab comes to him. When the king comes he says [to Elijah], "Art thou he that troubleth Israel?"

That is the way with men. They bring down the wrath of God upon themselves, and then blame God's people. A great many people are blaming God for these hard times. Look on the millions and millions of [dollars] spent for whiskey. Why, it is about time for famine to strike the land. If men had millions of [dollars], it wouldn't be long before all the manhood would be struck out of them.

Now, the people of Israel had gone over to Baal; they had forgotten the God that brought them out of Egypt— the God of Jacob and Abraham and of their fathers. "Now," said Elijah, "let's have this settled. Let some of your people make an offering to their God on Mount Carmel, and I will make an offering to my God, and the God that answers by fire will be the God." The king agreed, and the day arrived. You could see a great stir among the people that day. They were moving up to Mount Carmel. By-and-by Ahab came up in his royal carriage, and those four hundred and fifty prophets of Baal and four hundred prophets of the groves made a great impression. Dressed in priestly robes, they moved solemnly up that mountain. The king swept along in his chariot, and, perhaps, passed by the poor priest Elijah, who came slowly up, leaning upon his staff, his long white hair streaming about his shoulders. People don't believe in sensations. That was one of the greatest sensations of their age. What was going to happen? No doubt the whole nation

242

had been talking about this Elijah, and when he came to that mountain, the crowd looked upon him as the man who held the key of heaven. When he came up he addressed the children of Israel. Perhaps there were hundreds of thousands. "How long halt ye between two opinions? If the Lord be God follow him: but if Baal, then follow him. And the people answered him not a word." Their eight hundred and fifty prophets had made a great impression upon them, and the king was afraid too.

These people are just like a great many people now. They are afraid to go into the inquiry room for what people will say. If they do go in they get behind a post, so that they can't be seen. They are afraid the people in the store will find it out, and make fun of them. Moral courage is wanted by them, as it was wanted by [the Israelites]. How many among us have not the moral courage to come out for the God of their mothers? They know these black-hearted hypocrites around them are not to be believed. They know these men who scoff at their religion are not their friends, while their mothers will do everything for them. The truest friends we can have are those who believe in Christ.

> "And the people answered him not a word. Then said Elijah unto the people, I, even I only, remain a prophet of the LORD; but Baal's prophets are four hundred and fifty men. Let them therefore give us two bullocks; and let them choose one bullock for themselves, and cut it in pieces, and lay it on wood, and put no fire under: and I will dress the other bullock, and lay it on wood, and put no fire under: And call ye on the name of your gods, and I will call on the name of the LORD: and the God that answereth by fire, let him be God. And all the people answered and said, It is well spoken" (1 Kgs. 18:21–24).

"Yes, sir, that's right. We'll stand by that decision." They built an altar, and laid their bullock on it, and began to cry to Baal, "O Baal! O Baal! Baal! Baal!" No answer. They cry louder and louder, but no answer comes. They pray from morning till noon, but not a sound. Elijah says, "Louder; you must pray louder. He must be on a journey; he must be asleep. He must be on a journey or asleep." They cry louder and louder. Some people say it doesn't matter what a man believes, so long as he is earnest. These men were terribly in earnest. No Methodists shout as they did. They cry as loud as their voices will let them, but no answer. They take their knives and cut themselves in their earnestness. Look at those four hundred and fifty prophets of Baal and four hundred prophets of the grove, all covered with blood, as they cry out in their agony. They have no God. Young man, who is your master? Whom do you serve? If you are serving Baal, I tell you if ever you get into trouble he will not answer you.

No answer came. Three o'clock came, the hour for the evening sacrifice, and Elijah prepared his altar. He would have nothing to do with the altar of Baal. He merely took twelve stones, representing the twelve tribes of Israel, and built his altar, and laid his bullock on. No doubt some skeptic said he had some fire concealed in his garment, for he dug a trench all around it to hold water. Then he told them to bring four barrels of water and emptied them over his sacrifice. Four more barrels were brought and thrown on the bullock, making eight, and then four barrels more were added, making twelve in all. Then, there lay that bullock, dripping with water, and Elijah came forward.

Every ear and eye was open. Those bleeding Baalites looked at him. What was going to be the end of it? He came forward, calm as a summer evening. He prayed to the God of Isaac and Abraham—when, behold, look! look! down it came—fire from the very throne of God, and consumed the wood and the stones and the sacrifice, and the people cried, "The Lord is the God!" The question was decided. The God that answereth by fire is the God of man. My friends, who is your God now? The God who answers prayer? Or have you no God?

I can imagine some of you saying, "If I had been on Mount Carmel and seen that I would have believed it." But I will tell you of a mount on which occurred another scene. That was a wonderful scene, but it does not compare with the scene on Calvary. Look there! God's own beloved Son hanging between two thieves and crying, "Father, forgive them, for they know not what they do." Talk about wonderful things. This has been the wonder of ages.

A man once gave me a book of wonderful things. I saw a good many wonders in it, but I did not see anything so wonderful in it as the story of the Cross. My friends, see His expiring look. See what happened. The very rocks were rent, the walls of the temple were rent, and all nature owned its God. The sun veiled its face and darkness fell over the earth when the Son of man expired on Mount Calvary. Where can you find a more wonderful sight than this? Those Israelites lived on the other side of the Cross; we live on this side of it.

If a man wants proof of His gospel look around this assembly. See men who thirty days ago were slaves, bound hand and foot to some hellish passion which was drawing them to hell. What a transformation there is. All things seem changed to them. They have got a new nature. "Is not this the power of God?" said a young convert to me today, "It seems as if we were living in the days of miracles, and the Son of God is coming down and giving men complete victory over lusts and passions." That is what the Son of God does for men, and yet, with all the proofs before their eyes, men are undecided.

What is it that keeps you from your decision? I wish I had time to tell you many of the reasons. Hundreds of thousands of men are thoroughly convinced, but they lack moral courage to come out and confess their sins.

Others are being led captive by some sin. They have got some [particular] sin, and as long as they hold on to it there is no hope. A man the other day said he would like to become a Christian, but he had a bet upon the election, and he wanted that settled first. He did not think that he might die before that was decided. Eternity is drawing on. Suppose we die without God, without hope, without everlasting life: it seems to me it would have been better never to have been born. My friends, I ask you tonight, why not come out like men? Say, "Cost what it will, I will accept Jesus tonight." Now, have moral courage. Come. How many of you are thoroughly convinced in your minds that you ought to be Christians tonight? Now just ask yourselves the question: "What hinders me, what stands in my way?" I can imagine some of you looking behind you to see how the one sitting there looks. If he seems serious, you look serious; if he laughs, you will laugh and come to the conclusion that you'll not accept Him tonight. You think of your companions, and you say you cannot stand their jeers. Is not that so? Come. Trample the world under your feet and take the Lord tonight, cost what it will. Say, "By the grace of God I will serve Him from this hour." Turn your backs upon hell, and set your faces toward heaven, and it will be the best night of your lives.

Have you ever seen a man who accepted Christ regret it? You cannot find a man who has changed masters and gone over to Christ who has regretted it. This is one of the strongest proofs of Christianity. Those who have never followed Him only regret it. I have seen hundreds dying when in the army and when a missionary, and I never saw a man who died conscious but who regretted that he had not lived a Christian life.

My friends, if you accept Him tonight it will be the best hour of your life. Let this night be the best night of your lives. Let me bring this to your mind: if you are lost it will be because you do not decide. "How long halt ye between two opinions? if the LORD be God, follow him: but, if Baal, then follow him." How many men in this assembly want to be on the Lord's side? Those who want to take their stand on the side of the true God rise. (Upon this request by Mr. Moody nearly two thousand men instantly arose.)

The ministry of Christ was to call sinners to repentance and provide a means for their salvation, as Moody points out early in this sermon. Jesus attracted large crowds, and people of many backgrounds were confronted with the gospel message: every person is a sick sinner, and Jesus Christ is the great Physician who has come to heal our sickness. It doesn't matter who or what you are; the need is the same.

The remainder of the sermon focuses on the spiritual needs of prostitutes. Moody apparently has a unique concern for them. He makes it clear in his sermon that Jesus spent time with sinful women and they accepted Him as Savior. Moody points out that the prostitutes of his day need help from Christians, and if Jesus was willing to interact with them, so should Christian women be willing to go into the brothels to share their faith with prostitutes and point them to a better life. Moody's concern was evident to many prostitutes, and many were converted.

The sermon ends with the reading of a letter from a woman who confirms the idea that she and others like her wanted release from their lifestyle, but they needed the help of Christians to show them the way.

Though Moody preached the need for spiritual restoration, he never forgot the importance of social involvement. In his mind the two worked together as tools for improving the plight of individuals here on earth. Throughout his life he devoted much time and money to causes that would bring peace and comfort to those in great need, both spiritually and physically.

CHAPTER FIFTEEN

Sinners Called to Repentance

I want to call your attention tonight to a text which you will find in the fifth chapter of Luke and thirty-second verse. The text is also recorded in Matthew and in Mark, and whenever you find a passage recorded by all three of the evangelists you may know that it is one of those important truths which He wants to impress upon people. "I came not to call the righteous, but sinners to repentance." It was when He first came down to Capernaum that He uttered these words. He had been cast out of Nazareth; they didn't want Him; they wouldn't have salvation. And He came down to Capernaum, and there He found Levi sitting at the receipt of customs, and He called him to become one of His disciples. Levi was so full of joy when he found Christ—as all young converts are—that he got up a great feast, and he invited all the publicans and sinners to it. I suppose he wanted to get them all converted—that was the reason he prepared a sumptuous feast. It was not to hear Jesus, but just to partake of the feast that Levi had prepared for them. And Jesus was there too among these publicans and sinners. The Pharisees were there too, and they began to murmur against His disciples, saying, "Why do these men eat with publicans and sinners?" and it was on this occasion that Christ uttered this wonderful text: "I came not to call the righteous, but the sinners to repentance." That is what He came into this world for; He came into the world just for the very purpose of saving sinners.

Now a good many men come to Chicago to do a certain work. Some come to practice law; that's their profession. Others come to practice medicine, because that's their business; some are businessmen and some are mechanics. And when Christ came into this world He came for a purpose; He had a profession, if you will allow me the expression—He came to call sinners to repentance.

You know when He was going down to the Samaritan town His disciples went down to see whether they would let Him come there. We find Him on His way from Galilee to Jerusalem. You know there was such a hatred between the Jews and the Samaritans that they would have no dealings with each other, and He sent His disciples on to see if He would be allowed to enter. The Samaritans would not allow Him there, and His disciples were so incensed that James and John asked Jesus to "command fire to come down from heaven and consume them, even as Elias did." "Why," said the Son of man, "I didn't come to destroy men's lives, but to save them." That's what He came for. He came to bless men; He came to do men good, and there is not a sinner here tonight who cannot be saved and will be saved tonight if they wish.

You may call this world a great hospital, and all the people are born sick. A great many people imagine their souls are never diseased, who think they don't need a physician; but when people wake up to the fact that their souls are diseased, then they find the need of a physician. But there is no need for the physician unless you feel you are sick. You know you could not send a physician to a man who was well. Suppose I go [to] the West Side and ask a celebrated physician to come over and see Mr. White. Suppose he comes round and finds Mr. White sitting in his drawing room perfectly well. "Why, how is this? Mr. Moody told me you were sick, and bade me make a professional call." Not only is the physician disgusted but the patient is too. The world doesn't send for a physician till sickness comes. When it feels sick then it sends for a doctor, and the doctor comes. And whenever a man feels his need of Christ and calls, that moment he comes and is healed. There is a Physician here tonight for every sinner; I don't care what your sins may be, or how long you have been living in sin; I don't care if your life has been as black as hell, the great Physician is here. What for? Just to heal every man and woman that wants to be healed.

Now, the great trouble is to make people believe they are sick; but the moment you believe that you are, then it is that you are willing to take the remedy. I remember some years ago a patent medicine came out, and the whole of Chicago was placarded about it. I could not turn my head but I saw "Paine's Painkiller." On the walls, on the curbstones, everywhere was "painkiller," "painkiller." I felt disgusted at the sight of these bills constantly telling me about this patent medicine. But one day I had a terrible headache, so bad that I could hardly see, and was walking down the streets and saw the bills again and went and bought some. When I was well I didn't care for it, but when I got sick I found it was the very thing I wanted. If there is one here who feels the need of a Savior, remember the greater the sin the greater the need of a Savior.

I remember when I was coming back from Europe on the steamer there was a young officer; I felt greatly drawn toward him because I could see he was dying. It didn't seem to him as if he was dying, but you know death is very deceitful. He seemed to be joyous and lighthearted. He would talk about his plans, and take out his guns, and tell how he intended to go hunting when he arrived; but it seemed to me that he would not live to see this country. By-and-by he was taken down on his bed, and then the truth came to him that death was upon him. He got a friend to write out a telegram, which this friend was to send to his mother when they arrived. It read: "Mother, I am real sick.—Charlie." As soon as the boat touched the shore he was to send it. "But," said someone, "why not tell her in the telegram to come?" "Ah," he replied, "she will come." He knew whenever she read it and saw that he wanted help, she would come. It was the knowledge of his need that would bring her.

So Christ is waiting to hear our need, and man's need brings out the help of God. As I said before, the real trouble is that men don't think they need Him. You know that in one place—in the fifteenth chapter of Luke—they brought this charge against Him: "This man receiveth sinners, and eateth with them." This charge was brought against Him again and again. I am told by Hebrew scholars that instead of "receiveth" it should be rendered, "He is looking out for them." And that's what He was doing. He was looking out for them. He didn't care how black in sin they might be, He was ready to take them.

Now, a great many say, "I am too great a sinner to be saved." That is like a hungry man saying he is too hungry to eat, or a sick man saying he is too sick to send for a doctor, or a beggar saying, "I am too poor to beg; I'll wait till I get some money first." If a man is hungry and perishing, you must relieve him.

Now there is not a sinner in Chicago but has his representative in the Bible. Take, for instance, the publicans. You know the Jews thought this class about the lowest in the world. They put them lower than any other kind of sinner. They placed them along with the sinners— "publicans and sinners." The publicans were the tax collectors, and they defrauded the people at every turn. For instance, a man in South Chicago will pay [more than], perhaps, a hundred thousand dollars for the privilege of just collecting the taxes, and then he goes to work and screws the people out of a hundred and fifty thousand dollars. He doesn't care a straw for justice or appearances. He comes into the cottage of the widow and taxes half [of all] she has. At every house the tax collector puts the blocks to his victims, and famine often comes in when he goes out. The people detest him; they hate him with a perfect hatred. They always find him a drag on them, and [they] feel he hasn't a bit of sympathy for them. Their money, they find, is taken without warrant; their homes are broken up, and trouble and starvation come on them. And so the [Jewish] publican was hated wherever he turned. He was the agent of the Roman tyrant, and the people were brought up to shun him. He deserved it all, and even more, by his heartless exactions; and yet Christ forgave even him. And just so rumsellers can be saved. And another class that Christ had mercy on was the thieves when, on the cross, he saved a thief. There may be some thief here tonight. I tell you, my friend, you may be saved if you only will. There may be someone here who is persecuting a good wife, and making her home a perfect hell on earth. But you, too, may be saved. There may be some here persecuting the church, but there's salvation for you. When Saul was persecuting the Christians from city to city, he was stopped short by the voice of God; he was converted. And those high-headed Pharisees, so well versed in the law of Moses, even they were converted—Joseph of Arimathea was a Pharisee, and so was Nicodemus.

But tonight I want to talk about another class that Jesus dealt with and led to a higher life. I want to talk about fallen women. There are some people who believe that these have fallen so low that Christ will pass them by. But my friends, that thought comes from the evil one.

In all this blessed Book there is not one, not a solitary one of this class mentioned that ever came to Him but that He received them. Yes, He even went out of His way and sought [them] out.

Now I want to take three representative cases where these women had to do with Christ. One is the case of an awakened one. The Spirit of God has dealt with her anxious, awakened soul. The Lord was one day at Jerusalem and a banquet was given [for] Him by Simeon. There was a banquet table in the house, arranged according to the fashion of that day. Instead of chairs for the guests, the guests sat reclining on lounges, as was customary. Well, it was just one of these repasts that our Lord sat down to, along with the wealthy Simeon and his many guests. But no sooner had He entered than this woman followed Him into the house and fell down at His feet and began to wash them with her tears. It was the custom in those days to wash one's feet on entering a house. Sandals were worn and the practice was necessary. Well, this woman had gotten into the house by some means and once inside had quietly stolen up to the feet of Jesus. And in her hands she brought a box; but her heart too, was just as full of ointment as the box she carried. And there was the sweetest perfume as she stole to His feet. And her tears started to fall down on those sacred feet; hot, scalding tears that gushed out like water. She said nothing while the tears fell, and then she took down her long, black hair and wiped His feet with the hair of her head. And after that she poured out the ointment on His feet. Then straightway the Pharisees began talking together.

How all through the New Testament these Pharisees kept whispering and talking together! They said, shaking their heads, "This man receiveth sinners"; and then, "This man, if he were a prophet, would have known who and what manner of woman this is that toucheth him: for she is a sinner." No prophet, they insisted, would allow that kind of a woman near Him but would push her away. And then the Savior read these thoughts and quickly rebuked them. He said, "Simeon, I have somewhat to say unto thee." And he said, "Master, say on." And He said, "Seest thou this woman? I entered into thine house, thou gavest me no water for my feet: but she hath washed my feet with tears, and wiped them with the hairs of her head. Thou gavest me no kiss: but this woman since the time I came in hath not ceased to kiss my feet. My head with oil thou didst not anoint: but this woman hath anointed my feet with ointment." Simeon was like a great many Pharisees nowadays, who say, "Oh, well, we will entertain that minister if we must. We don't want to—he's a dreadful nuisance—but we will have to put up with him; it's our duty to be patronizing." Well, the Master said more to His entertainer: "There was a certain creditor, which had two debtors; the one owed five hundred pence, and the other fifty, and when he had nothing to pay"—mark that, sinner; the debtor had nothing to pay. There is no sinner in the world that can pay anything to cancel his debt to God. The great trouble is that sinners think they can pay, some of them seventy-five cents on the dollar, some even feel able to pay ninety-nine cents on the dollar, and the one cent that they are short, they think they can make that up some way. That is not the way; it is all wrong. You must throw all the debt on God. Some few perhaps, will only claim to pay twenty-five cents on the dollar, but they are not humble enough either; they can't begin to carry out their bargain. Why, sinner, you couldn't pay one-tenth part of a single mill of the debt you are under to Almighty God.

Now it says in this parable that they could not pay him anything—they had nothing to give and the creditor frankly forgave them both. "Now, Simeon," the Master asked, "which should love that man the most?" "I suppose," was the reply, "he that was forgiven the most." "Thou hast rightly judged; this woman loves much because she hath been forgiven much," and went on to tell Simeon all about her. I suppose he wanted to make it plainer to Simeon, and he turned to the poor woman and said, "Thy sins are forgiven"—all forgiven; not part of them, not half of them, but every sin from the cradle up, every impure desire or thought was blotted out for time and eternity, and He said, "Go in peace." Yes, truly, she went out in peace, for she went out in the light of heaven. With what brightness the light must have come down to her from those eternal hills—with what beauty it must have flashed on her soul. Yes, she came to the feet of the Master for a blessing, and she got it, and if there is a poor woman here tonight who wants a blessing, she will get it.

I want to call your attention to a thought right here. You have not got the name of one of those poor women. The three women who had fallen, who had been guilty of adultery, and had been blessed by Him, not one of them has been named. It seems to me as if it had been intended that when they got to heaven we should not know them—they will just mingle with the rest. Their names have not been handed down for eighteen hundred years. They have called Mary Magdalene a fallen woman, but bear in mind there is nothing in Scripture to make us understand that she was a poor, fallen woman, and I believe if she had been, her name would not have been handed down.

Now, the next woman was altogether different from the woman in Luke. She didn't come with an alabaster box, seeking a blessing. She was perfectly indifferent; she was a careless sinner. Perhaps there are some poor fallen women who have come tonight in a careless spirit—only out of curiosity. They don't want a Savior; they don't want their sins blotted out; they don't want any forgiveness. Perhaps she had heard that at Moody and Sankey's they were going to preach repentance and that a great many fallen women were likely to be there and thought she would just come down to see how they took it.

Now you have a representative here. After Christ had that interview with Nicodemus, we are told He went up to Galilee by Samaria. He could have gone up to Galilee without going to Samaria, but He knew there was a fallen woman there. He got to the well and sent off His disciples to get bread. Why did He not keep one with Him? Because He knew the woman was coming that way, and she probably would not like to see so many. While He sat on the curbstone of the well, a poor fallen woman of Samaria came along for water. You know the people in those days used to come out in the morning and evening to get their water, not in the blaze of the noonday sun. No doubt she was ashamed to come out there to meet the pure and virtuous at the well, and that was the reason why she stole out at that hour.

She brought her waterpot to get water, and when she came up the Master stopped her and asked her for a drink, just to draw her out. She saw He was a Jew. (We can always tell a Jew: God has put a mark upon them.) "How is this? You a Jew and ask a Samaritan for a drink? The Jews have no dealings with the Samaritans." "Ah, you don't know Me," He replied; "if you would have asked Me for a drink I would have given you living water." "How could you give me living water? Why, you have no vessel to draw water with." "Whosoever drinketh of this water shall thirst again, but whosoever shall drink of the water that I shall give him will have a well springing up in his heart into everlasting life." "Well," probably she thought, "that is a good thing. One draft of water will give me a well—one draft of water for the rest of my days." She asked Him for this living water, and He told her, "Go, bring thy husband." He was just drawing her out, just getting her up to the point of confession. "I have no husband," she said. "For thou hast had five husbands, and he whom thou now hast is not thy husband; in that saidst thou truly." I can see that woman's astonishment. She looks all around to see who had told Him all about her. [This is] like a man who came up from Michigan lately, who came into the tabernacle and listened to the sermon which, as he told me, seemed all to be preached at him. He wondered who had told me all about him. He got Christ, and is going back to Michigan to preach the gospel of Jesus Christ.

The Word of God reached her, and she saw she was detected. "Sir, I perceive thou art a prophet"; then she went on the old religious discussion, but the Lord turned her from that and told her that the hour had come when the people must worship the Father in spirit and in truth, not in this or that particular mountain, nor yet in Jerusalem. And she said, "When the Messiah cometh He will tell us all things," and when she had said this she was ready for the truth. Then Jesus said, "I am the Messiah."

Just then she saw His disciples coming, and probably she thought these men might know who she was, and she got up her pot, and away she went to the city. The moment she got within the gates she shouted, "Come see this man I have met at the well. Is not this the Messiah? Why, He has told me all that ever I did." And you can see all the men, women, and children running out of that city up to the well. As He stands in the midst of His disciples and He sees the multitudes coming running toward them, He says, "Look yonder; look at the fields, for they are already white with the harvest; look what that poor fallen woman has done." And He went into that town as an invited guest, and many believed on account of the woman's testimony, and many more believed on account of His own.

Now, my friends, He did not condemn the poor adulteress. The Son of God was not ashamed to talk with her and tell her of that living water, those who drank of which, He said, would never die. He did not condemn her. He came to save her, came to tell how to be blessed here and blessed hereafter.

The next case is still much worse. You may say it is like black, blacker, blackest, compared with the other two. I want to speak about this one that is in the eighth chapter of John. One woman I have spoken of was in the house of a Pharisee at a dinner party, the other by the well of Sychar, and now we come to the temple porch. They have taken a woman in adultery, have caught her in the very act. They have not gotten the man; they have held only the poor woman. While He is speaking, the Pharisees are driving this poor fallen woman right into the temple. What a commotion there would be here tonight, if such a scene should take place in the tabernacle!

She had broken the law of Moses, by which a woman caught in the act of adultery was to be put to death. The woman is brought toward Him, and now they are about to put the question of her life or death before Him. He had said that He hadn't come to condemn the world, but to save the world, and they are just going to try and condemn Him by His own words. They say to Him, "Moses in the law commandeth us, that such should be stoned: what sayest thou?" But not a word did He speak. Jesus stooped down and wrote on the ground, as though He hadn't heard them. We don't know what He wrote. Perhaps, "Grace and truth come by Jesus Christ." Perhaps He wrote that. But while He thus busied Himself they cried out the louder, demanding an answer to their question. So at length He lifted Himself up and said, "He that is without sin among you, let him first cast a stone at her." Never did an answer so completely serve its purpose; you who never were guilty of an offense, just you cast the first stone. And, amid the strangest silence He again stooped and wrought with His finger on the ground. This time, perhaps, He wrote, "I am not come to call the righteous, but sinners to repentance." And soon

He rose again, but ere He did so He heard the patter of retreating feet on the pavement and when now He glanced up, He saw none but the woman. One by one they had been convicted by their own conscience, and slunk away; not one of them there could throw the stone. And the Savior looked at the woman. I can imagine the tears coming trickling down her cheeks as Jesus Christ, in kindest tones, asked her, "Woman, where are those thine accusers? hath no man condemned thee?" And for an instant she could not answer.

Who knows how that poor soul had reached her sad plight! Perhaps one of those very Pharisees who had left her had led her astray. The very man who had clamored loudest to condemn her was likely the guilty one. And there she stood alone; the betrayer was left untouched, as too often he is today—a miserable, unjust, untrue sentiment, by which the man, who is equally guilty, is received in society and the woman is condemned. But at last she gained her voice and said, "No man, my Lord," and then, perhaps, told how her parents had died when she was very young. A stepmother, perhaps, had taken her and treated her harshly, and then had turned her adrift [in] the world. Or perhaps a drunken father had turned home into darkness, and she had been driven from it almost brokenhearted; and so in her helplessness her innocent affections were gained, and then she had been led astray. The Master knew it all, and when He heard her reply He said, "Neither do I condemn thee; go, and sin no more." She had been dragged into the temple to be stoned, but now Christ had delivered her. She came to be put to death, but she received life everlasting.

My friends, the Son of God will not now condemn any poor fallen woman that leaves off her sins and just casts herself down at His feet. He will take you up just as you are. When [I was] in Philadelphia, a fallen woman came into the inquiry room and threw herself down on the floor. The Christian helpers talked and talked to her but couldn't get a word out of her; they couldn't do a thing with her. The Honorable George H. Steward came to me, and said, "We wish you would come, we don't know what to make of her." She was weeping bitterly, and, as far off as I was, I could hear her sobs all over the room. So I went and said, "What is the trouble?" At last she spoke, and the bitterness of her despairing voice went to my heart. "I have fallen from everything pure, and God cannot save me; there is no hope." I told her tenderly that God could still lift her up and save her. I said, "Are you only just willing to be forgiven? A merciful Father is waiting and longing to pardon." She said at last she could not abandon her course, as no one would give her a home. But that difficulty was gotten round by my assuring her [that] kind friends would provide for her; and then she yielded, and that same day was given a pleasant place in the home of a Presbyterian minister. But for forty-eight hours after entering her new home that poor, reclaimed woman cried, day and night, and we went for her mother, and on hearing our story the mother clasped her hands and cried, "Has my daughter really repented? Thank God for His mercy; my heart has just been breaking. I've prayed so long for her without result; take me to her." And that reformed daughter of sin has lived consistently ever since, and when I was last in Philadelphia she was one of the most esteemed members in that Presbyterian church.

And so every one of you can begin anew, and God will help and man will help you. Oh, turn, and do not die. Seven short years is the allotted life of a fallen woman. Oh, escape your early doom, escape your infamy, and hear God's voice calling you to repent. Your resolution to amend will be borne up by hosts of friends; never fear for that. Just take the decided step, and you will be helped by every good man and woman in the community. Oh, I beseech you to act right now and settle this great question for time and eternity.

I heard of a mother whose daughter was led astray, and the poor daughter tried to hide herself, thinking her mother would not forgive her. The mother went to the town where she supposed her child had gone, but she hunted and hunted unsuccessfully. The trouble with most of those girls who go astray is they go under assumed names, and this daughter had done the same thing, and that mother couldn't find her. At last she found a place where fallen women resorted to, and the mother went to the keeper of that place and begged her to let her hang up her picture in the room, and consent was granted. Hundreds of fallen women came into that room and carelessly glanced at the picture and went out. Weeks and months rolled on, until at length one night a poor fallen girl came into the room. She was going out as carelessly as she had entered, when her eye caught the picture, and, gazing at it for a moment, she burst into a flood of tears. "Where did you get it?" she sobbed. They told her how her mother came there, heart-broken, and asked to have her picture hung up in that room, in the hope of finding her daughter. The girl's memory went back to her days of peace and purity, recalling the acts of kindness of that loved mother, and she then and there resolved to return. See how that mother sought for her and forgave her.

Oh, poor fallen ones, the Son of God is seeking for you tonight. If you haven't got a mother to pray for you, the Son of God wants to be everything to you. He wants to receive you to Himself. Let me hold Him up to you as your best Friend. He wants to take you to His loving bosom, and this very night and very hour you can be raised if you will.

There was a woman who was trying to get a poor girl to go back to her home. She said, "Neither my mother, my father, nor my brothers will forgive me. They won't permit me to go back." "Will you give me your address?" the lady asked. The address was obtained, and the very next post brought a letter marked "immediately," and it seemed as if the whole hearts of her father and mother and brothers were poured out in that letter. It was filled with kindness and urged her to come home and all would be forgotten. There is many a poor fallen girl in Chicago whose mother is praying for her, and whose heart is aching because she won't go back. Your mother will forgive you, and all your friends, if you will only show true signs of repentance. They will take you home.

O my friends, let this be the last night you will live in sin—in shame. Let this be your last night in which you will live in sin. Take those sins you have to Him, and He will forgive you. He has said, "Let the wicked forsake his ways," and pardon is ready. That is what our Lord will do. He will pardon you and make you pure. Will you let Him pardon you tonight?

Just before coming down this evening I received a letter from a fallen woman. I've received a number during the past few days. Thank God the spirit is at work among that class! And let me say right here, if there is any person here who keeps a brothel, if you will allow Christian ladies admittance, they will go gladly and hold meetings. This idea that Christian ladies do not care for your class is false—as false as the blackest lie that ever came out of hell. Why, some of the first ladies of the city have lately been visiting these houses personally, and [they] have been trying to save their erring sisters. A few days ago, several came to me and asked if I couldn't get a list of all the brothels in the city. I went to police headquarters and got the names of the keepers and addresses and gave it to these Christian women. And since then, many houses have been visited. These charges that Christian women will not have them in their homes are equally false. The other night a lady of culture was on her knees with a poor one who told the lady that she was a fallen girl and did not know where to go if she didn't go back to her brothel. "Come and stay at my house," said the lady, "I will take care of you," and when the girl got up from her knees, the lady saw she was a poor, colored girl. That good Christian kept her till she got her a good situation. Another one not long ago received the truth, and one of our ministers wrote to her parents, got a pass and sent her home to her forgiving parents. Let me ask you not to believe that we are cruel; that we are hard-hearted; that we do not care for the fallen women but only for the abandoned men. We have a place to shelter you, and if that is not large enough, the businessmen will put up another. They will do everything for you if you are only repentant; they will not try to keep you down and cast you off. If you are sincere, there are hundreds and thousands of people in this city whose hearts will go out to you. But I want to read this letter:

CHICAGO, Dec. 14.

Mr. Moody—Many fallen women in this city would, in these days, gladly change their mode of life and seek Christ and restoration to the homes and hearts of parents and friends whom they, weakly, left many, many bitter years and months ago, if only they could see some way to an honorable living and friendly recognition and help when they should seek these.

Now, let me say here that any young woman who wants reclamation ought not to look into the future. Say to yourselves, "I will be saved tonight, come what will."

You say, "Seek first the kingdom of Christ"; but, my dear brother (for such you seem even to me), why do this if only returning shame awaits us?

I wish every fallen woman would think as this one does; why, I would be a brother to you all. Thank God, I've got a brother's heart for all of you. I wish every one of you would feel that I want to do you good—that I only want to lift you up.

Suppose a hundred fallen women of this city were at the tabernacle tonight—no doubt more than this number will be there—and that these should seek Christ and find forgiveness, for you assure us there is full forgiveness for even us, so that these scarlet stains should be "whiter than snow"—where, I ask, shall we live? What shall we do?

We must return ere the echo of the last prayer in that tabernacle has died away, to the apartments which have only known our bitter shame and again meet the devil in his chosen home.

Let me say, again, that no woman in this audience need do that. There will be homes open for you. God will provide for you if you will trust Him. I hope there will be hundreds here tonight who will say, "I will never return to that place. I will never go back to that house of shame; I will never meet the devil in those homes more; I will rather die in the poorhouse than do it; I turn my back forever upon death and hell."

No home of parent or friend, or praying Christian who joined in your prayer at the tabernacle for us, would offer our weary bodies shelter there, or our willing hands labor wherewith honest bread might be earned. No Christian's purse affords tomorrow's bread.

Dear friends, let the morrow take care of itself. Don't be looking at the future. Just walk by faith. That's what every Christian must do.

The very ones who came here to pray for us go away scorning us; and while with the virtuous wife and mother and the pure maiden we would plead a common Savior, they would thrust us from them. What can we do? Who will help us?

There remains only a life of shame and an unwept death, physical and eternal, for us. Hopelessly,

"ONE OF THEM"

This is the core of the gospel: Christ was the sacrifice for our sins. And because of His death, provision was made that all can be saved.

This sermon traces the final hours of Christ before His death on the cross. After Judas leaves the room where the last supper is taking place, Christ tells His other disciples about heaven in order to comfort them. Later we find Him praying in the darkness for the stability of His followers and for the completion of His work according to the Father's will.

His betrayal was painful for it involved Judas, a disciple whom He trusted. When we today turn our backs on Christ, He is equally hurt, for such a response is an act of rejection.

He is led away, tried, and executed, yet Jesus' execution was not final. His resurrection marked the beginning of life for those who repent. Christ died for our sins, and it is time we accepted His work on our behalf.

CHAPTER SIXTEEN

The Sacrifice of Christ

You will find my text tonight in the fifteenth chapter of First Corinthians, and part of the third verse: "Christ died for our sins according to the Scriptures." I was going to preach in the city of Dublin a few years ago, and the town was placarded giving notice of the meeting. There was one passage of Scripture at the bottom of the bill that my eye rested upon: "Christ died for our sins." I had read it a great many times, but I seemed to see it now in a new light, and that light flashed into my soul as it never did before: "Christ died for *my* sins." That's the way to put it—"for *my* sins." And I wish I could get everyone here to take it that way and just keep saying it while I preach to you tonight: "Christ died for me."

My friends, will you only make this personal and re-member that He died for you? Let that little boy and girl remember that He died for you just as much as for that gray-headed man, and let those who came in to scoff at the meeting remember that the text is for them—that Christ died for you. I have often thought that if I could only make people feel this really, and could tell the story

271

of His death as it ought to be told, I would only preach one sermon and go up and down the world and just tell this one story. I don't know anything that would break the heart of the world like this story if it could be brought before men and women and they would feel it. I know it broke my heart, and I have often thought if I could tell it as it ought to be told, I would be the happiest man in the world. I don't believe it has ever been told yet. I don't believe the man has been born who could tell it; I don't believe that the angels in heaven could tell it. Sometimes people say we have over-drawn the pictures in the Bible, but there is one story that has never been over-drawn—the story of His death. No one ever did justice to that story; no one ever made that real. I believe the heart of every man in this audience would be broken if I could make that story real.

I remember during the war how I would take up a paper and read about the great battles and loss of life; but I would lay down the paper and soon forget all about the thousands that had been slain. But I went into the war and was at the battles of Fort Donelson and Pittsburgh Landing. After I came home and began to read the papers and see the accounts of the great battles, the whole thing would come up before me. I could hear their dying groans; I could hear them crying for their mothers, their appeals for water. The whole thing was real, and the whole trouble is that most people take up this story of the Bible and don't make it real. They look upon it as the old story of eighteen hundred years ago which they have heard from their cradle. I remember I went five hundred miles to Dublin to attend a meeting, and when I got there the preacher got up and began to talk about the death of Christ. "Well," I said, "he should give us something new." But when I went home to the house where I was staying there were two old pilgrims sitting, and they were talking about the sermon and the death of Christ. The tears were trickling down their cheeks, and they spoke about the event as if Christ had died in Dublin that afternoon. I felt rebuked, ashamed at myself that those old men should speak so lovingly about this event, while I had treated it so lightly. I believe [that] if we were living as we ought to, it would be fresh every night, every hour, of our lives.

Now tonight I propose to take up the last hours of Christ before He went to Calvary. You know we love to hear the last words of our friends. I remember a few weeks ago, when I went to look upon the dead face of my eldest brother, how earnestly I inquired, "What were his last words?"—how I went round the places where he had been, and how for days I tried to pick up what he had said to this and that man, and how I treasured up his last words. And it seems to me every Christian ought to linger round the cross and pick up the loving words of our Savior and treasure them up. So tonight I want you just to go back nineteen hundred years. Let us forget we are living here in Chicago. Let us go back and imagine we are living in the land of Palestine—at Jerusalem; and let us just think we are walking down the streets of Jerusalem.

It is on a Thursday afternoon, and we see thirteen men coming down the street. Every eye is upon them. The boys are opening their eyes at them. Men, women, and children are running out of their houses to see those men. Let us imagine we are strangers, and we ask who these men are, and they tell us, "Why, that's the Galilean prophet and His apostles, from the city of Capernaum." We look upon them with amazement. We have heard how that man has given sight to the blind, how He has cured the lepers, given bread to the hungry, and raised the dead. The whole land has been full of Him, and out of curiosity we follow the little band. They go along the narrow streets, and come to a common-looking house and enter and ascend a flight of stairs. Suppose we go up those stairs with them; we find them there in a guest chamber, the great Prophet seated with His twelve apostles. We are told He became exceeding sorry. He was soon to taste the bitter cup, to taste death for every man, to lay down His innocent life for the guilty, the just for the unjust, and then He is exceeding sorry. His soul is troubled, and as He sits there at that table He lets out the secret of His heart, and tells them that that night He is going to be betrayed by one of them. They look at one another, and one says, "Lord, is it I?" "No." And another says, "Master, is it I?" "No," and they one after another put the question till it comes to Judas. And that black-hearted traitor, the devil who has already been at the high priest's, turns to Him and says, "Is it I?" and the Lord says, "Thou hast said it; and what thou doest do it quickly." That ought to have broken his black heart, but it didn't; and he arose and went out of that chamber.

Hear him as he goes down those stairs and into that dark night—we are told that it was the darkest the world ever saw. That night the Son of man was to be betrayed by man. He went off to the Sanhedrin, to the chief priests, and he sold Him—sold Him very cheap, my friends—sold Him for some fifteen or twenty dollars. How many men today are selling Him as cheaply— selling him for a song! They don't want Him. A woman told me last night, "I don't want Him; I wouldn't take Him as a gift." She told me with her own lips that she would rather go to hell than heaven. Oh, what a heart! I hope if there is a hard-hearted person in this building like her, their heart will be broken tonight.

But while Judas was out selling his Master, Jesus was speaking tender words to His disciples. What a tender parting! For three years He had been associated with that holy band; they had walked with the blessed Master, and heard those wonderful parables; they had seen Him raise people from the dead, had seen Him cure the deaf, the dumb, and the blind—they had been in His company for three years, and now they were about to be separated for a time, and it was on this occasion He uttered those memorable words: "Let not your heart be troubled."

They were now by themselves, the traitor had gone out. "Ye believe in God, believe also in me. In my Father's house are many mansions; if it were not so I would have told you. I go to prepare a place for you." There was the Master in that dark hour; in that bitter, supremely bitter hour, trying to cheer and comfort the little band. And then He uttered that wonderful prayer recorded in the seventeenth chapter of John. He poured his heart out to God in prayer. He not only prayed for His disciples, that had stood firmly by His side, but prayed for His enemies. And afterward He said, "The hour of my departure is at hand."

And then He gathered the eleven around Him and they started out of the house and went down through the streets of Jerusalem. They went out through the eastern gate, passed over through the outlying space down to the Valley of Jehoshaphat, and so to the garden of Gethsemane. And there he took Peter and James and John and went on with them a little way apart, and then [He] withdrew about a stone's throw off from them and fell on His knees and began to pray.

You can hear Him in that cold night in that garden; you can hear His piercing cry: "Father, let this cup pass from me if it be thy will." It was the prayer of agony, and He sweat, as it were, great drops of blood. Oh, the agony the Son of God passed through that night, not only physical agony, but a greater mental agony, because the sins of the world lay on Him. He bore in His person the sin of the whole world, and God the Father turned His face away from Him because God could not look upon sin. The Father had to turn His face away from Him: He could not take away the cup, but He had to leave Him drink it to the very dregs for you and me. And Peter and James and John fell asleep; they could not watch one single hour with Him. And so while they thus slept and Christ was wrestling in prayer, a band of men came on the scene. They came on with lanterns and torches, as if they were hunting for someone. Jesus well knew who they were seeking. He woke up His disciples and went to the band and said, "Whom seek ye?" And they said, "We seek Jesus of Nazareth." Then said Jesus, "I am he," and there was something so mysterious about His person, something so wonderful about His face, that they were struck with awe. They trembled and felt as dead men and could not touch Him. And then Judas stepped out from the band. We don't know but he put his arm around the Savior's neck. Ah, what a lesson to professing Christians! Judas was near enough to the Lord to put his arms around His neck, and yet he went down to hell. Ah, you are not to know true men by their making the greatest professions; that kind doesn't always stand the highest but sometimes the very lowest. Then Judas went on and carried out his bargain. He may have put his arm around His neck, but at all events he kissed Him. Christ turned and said, "Judas, betrayest thou the Son of man with a kiss?" He may have said, "Professing to be my follower, do you betray me with a kiss?" He might have asked, "What have I done that you should betray me? Was I ever unkind; have I ever been untrue; have I ever deceived you; have I ever betrayed you? Why Judas, do I receive this treatment from you?" But he merely said, "Betrayest thou the Master with a kiss? What is it that thou hast done to agree to betray thy Master with a kiss?"

And then the men seized on Him and took those innocent hands that had been raised to bless people, that had brought bread to the hungry, had touched the leprous and made them clean, touched those that were blind and made them see, touched the deaf ears and hearts and made them hear and feel—those innocent hands that had been raised only to bless people, they took and bound them. And He resisted not. He gave himself up a willing sacrifice and was obedient to their will. And after they had bound Him they started back to the city with Him.

And they took Him to Annas, the father-in-law of Caiaphas, the high priest. And they brought Him in, and instead of waiting till the morning, the Sanhedrin was gathered hastily together. They were so thirsty for His blood they couldn't wait even a few hours. They hurried Him before the assembled Senate, where the first men of the nation were gathered together. Seventy of the rulers of the Jews came into the council that night. One after another they took their seats, and Caiaphas took his place at the head of the table. There they sat in solemn state, the highest court of the nation. And now they sought for witnesses to come and testify against Jesus. The law required that two men should agree together to establish any testimony. And at last they found two false witnesses that came and swore they heard Him talk against the holy temple, that He said they might destroy it and He could raise it up again in three days. Then, being questioned, He said, "Before Abraham was, I am." And being further questioned, He answered not a word. At last Caiaphas raised his voice and said, "I adjure thee by the living God, that thou tell us whether thou be the Christ the Son of God." And Jesus said unto him, "Thou hast said: nevertheless I say unto you, Hereafter shall ye see the Son of man sitting on the right hand of power, and coming in the clouds of heaven." And the moment Jesus said that, Caiaphas rent his clothes and said: "He hath spoken blasphemy; what further need have we of witnesses? Behold, now ye have heard his blasphemy!" Then he hurriedly put the question, "What think ye?" And they rendered as their verdict: "He is guilty of death." How the sentence rung out in that council chamber.

It was Thursday night; it may have been midnight.

Many of the citizens had retired, and it was not known until morning. The next day was a notable feast day. There were there people from all parts of the country; the whole city was crowded. Perhaps Zacchaeus was there from Jericho; perhaps many from whom He had cast out devils; perhaps blind Bartimaeus, no longer blind, was there, and that Samaritan woman Christ had met by the well of Sychar. Undoubtedly hundreds were there who, but for Jesus, could not have gotten there. Would they stand by Him? Would they cling to Him now, in this hour of His need? And Peter—he was of course there—would he be staunch? Only a few days before he had solemnly promised to stand by his Lord to the last. "Though others might deny Him, he would die with Him." Would not Peter, at least, have moral courage to come out before all the world and own Him? Alas, no. Why, that very night as Jesus was in the judgment hall, impetuous Peter denied Him with a curse, and swore he never knew Him. It seemed there was no hand to defend Him; no hand to help Him; there He was that night in the hands of His enemy.

Very early the next morning, at what hour we do not know, the officers of the governor came and bound Him and took Him away to Pilate to have Him put to death. The Romans had taken away the power of sentencing to death, and so the Jews could only put Him to death by gaining the Romans' consent. So now they brought Him to Pilate. Pilate never had such a person as that before him. He had sentenced many to death, but not like Him. He had often heard of this Galilean; His fame had long ago reached him. Strange rumors about Him had come up from Bethlehem. Perhaps Pilate had even seen Christ and talked with Him. Quite likely so, and his curiosity must have been excited by the many stories he heard about Him among his subjects. Pilate, this time, was with Christ two hours. At last he came out, after examining Him, and said, "I find no fault in this man." But the crowd cried out, "If you let this man go, you are not Caesar's friend." They knew this would touch his loyalty and ambition to be a successful politician. He could not, they argued, tolerate any rival to the Roman power, and his first duty would be to put down everything like rebellion. "If you don't condemn him, you are not Caesar's friend," rang in his ears, as the crowd insisted that Christ was a rebel and wanted to get up an insurrection in the land, and His friends wanted to make Him King. They raised their yells and ended by repeating, "You are no friend of Caesar's. We will report you at Rome, and you will lose your office." Poor Pilate! He hadn't moral courage to stand firm. And so he said, "This Jesus, is He a Galilean?" "Yes," they said, "he was brought up in Nazareth but has been living out in Galilee." So, the next thing, Pilate sent Him to Herod.

Now you can see that crowd moving through the city on their way to the Galilean's governor. When he saw Him he probably thought it was John, whom he had put to death, that had been raised from the grave, and curiosity [made him] excited to see. But when he found out who it really was, we are told he got out some cast-off garments, probably some that had belonged to one of their kings, and dressed Him in them, and, pointing their fingers in scorn at Him, [they] cried, "Hail, King of the Jews!" Then they blindfolded Him and struck Him on the head, saying in derision, "You are a prophet; tell us who struck you." Some would spit upon Him amid a torrent of scorn and contempt. Yes, my friends, they spat upon Him.

Suppose the Prince of Wales would come to this country, and someone would go up and spit upon him: why all Europe would be up about it. But when the Son of man came down to this earth they spat upon Him, and no one raised his voice against it. But with all this ignominy that bloodthirsty Herod, who took the life of John, refused to take His life, and sent Him back to Pilate. And now the crowd had increased. The whole city was excited. Everyone was talking about how the Galilean prophet had been brought before the Sanhedrin and found guilty of blasphemy, and was to die the terrible death of the cross. His friends, all the time He was on trial, not a solitary one stood up for Him. All forsook Him then. The very men who a few days before cried as He entered Jerusalem, "Hosannah, to the Son of David," now lifted up their voices and cried, "Away with Him!" "Crucify Him!"

And they brought Him back to Pilate, and undoubtedly around his house a crowd had gathered as great as that assembled here tonight. It didn't take much to rouse these Jews. They were very easily fired, and the whole city was aroused. They were clamoring—thirsty for His blood. Pilate was still anxious to release Him. His conscience told him to release Christ, and he also received a communication from his wife in which she said, "Have thou nothing to do with this just man, for I have suffered many things this day in a dream because of him." He tried to release Him, but he wanted to be on both sides. At last he said, "I've got a plan that will work, I think." It was customary, you know, to release a prisoner upon the day of the governor's feast, and he said, "I will get the vilest wretch I can, the blackest-hearted murderer and robber, and bring up this pure man and ask them which of the two they will have." But the chief priests heard what he was going to do, and went around among the crowd and told them and got their feelings worked up. And now Pilate thought he was going to get rid of the terrible responsibility of putting Him to death.

Picture the crowd standing around that governor's house. See the soldiers bringing out one with his hands dripping with the blood of his fellow man, and another who had all His life healed the sick, given life, and done good. "Which will I release unto you?" And they lift up their voices—it is the cry of the whole mob—"Barabbas,

Barabbas, Barabbas," and the poor governor, disappointed, cries out, "What shall I do with Christ?" "Let Him be crucified," that was the burden of the voice that rang through the streets of Jerusalem that day.

"Away with this pestilent fellow—we don't want him. Put him to death!" Pilate turned around and washed his hands with water and said, "I am innocent of the blood of this just person." Poor, blind, deceived man. He thought that he could wash his hands of this iniquitous decision; but what a mistake. When he had said this they cried, "His blood be upon us and on our children." Would to God they had cried out, "Let His blood be upon us and our children to save them," but that wasn't the cry. "Let His blood be upon us and on our children." And look what a punishment has come upon that race— see how they've been scattered to the four winds of heaven, because they neglected Him. Only about seventy years afterwards Titus came and besieged Jerusalem, and nearly 1,100,000 people perished, and ninety-seven thousand were sold to slavery. It fell, and the Jewish people have been wanderers for eighteen hundred years.

And then Pilate gave him up to be scourged. Now, I was a great many years a Christian before I knew what the Roman custom of scourging was, but when the truth dawned upon me, when I learned what it really was, I wept for days and got down on my knees and asked Him forgiveness for not loving Him more than I had. The custom of scourging consisted in taking the wrists and binding them tightly together and then fastening them to a post or pillar. The back was bared, and a lash, composed of sharp pieces of steel plaited together, was brought down upon the back. Oh, sinner, look at the prophet Isaiah, "He was wounded for our transgressions, he was bruised for our iniquities: the chastisement of our peace was upon him; and with his stripes we are healed." He was wounded for me. Yes, with His stripes am I healed. May this be a reality to everyone here tonight. Don't let us conceal it. It was the God of heaven they scourged for us. For fifteen minutes they brought down blow upon blow on that innocent body.

O you who cast Him away; you who see no reason why you should love Him; you who cannot see why you should take your stand on His side, why you should defend His cause, think of this! And after scourging Him, instead of binding up His wounds, and bringing oil and ointment and pouring it upon those wounds, instead of doing this they put upon Him some other cast-off garments and made Him a crown of thorns, and some wretch put it on His head.

You know when Queen Victoria sits on her throne, they put a crown upon her head filled with diamonds and precious stones worth about twenty million dollars; but here they crowned God's Son with a crown of thorns, the curse of the earth. And in mockery of a king, they put a stick in His hand. You know when the Queen of England sits on her throne she has a scepter in her hand; and here in the hands of the Prince of heaven they put a stick and scoffingly shouted, "Hail, King of the Jews!" They jeered and mocked that precious Christ. At last one of the crowd took the rod out of Jesus' hand and brought it down over His defenseless head, driving those thorns into His brow.

Oh, what treatment the Son of God received! And those wounds were made for us; He bore His stripes for you and for me. You can see the blood trickle down that innocent head, down that dear face, and over His bosom. And all for us! Oh, divine, infinite compassion: "He bore our sins in his own body on the tree." And now they take off the purple robe of scorn and put His own garment upon Him, and they lift up His cross and lay it upon Him. It is not a gilded cross, such as you ladies wear about the neck; it is not a cross of polished wood, thickly set with diamonds and precious stones, but a great, rugged, heavy cross, made roughly out of a tree.

Now, I see them lift and lay it on His shoulders. And they lay crosses on two thieves who are to be led away and executed with Him. The devil wanted to blacken the name of Christ, and so He was placed between two thieves who were made to carry their own crosses. Why the cross of Jesus was taken from His shoulders after a few steps, we can easily imagine. He cannot stand up—the sins of the whole world are piled upon Him—and He cannot stand up, much less walk under the accumulated load. See Him reel and stagger! See Him fall almost fainting to the earth! The mountain weight crushes down even the Son of God! They take the cross from His shoulders and lay it upon Simon the Cyrenian. And now look, sinners, and behold your Savior, behold the Lamb of God going up to Mount Calvary, like a sheep to the slaughter. Away to Calvary they are leading Him, to crucify and put Him to death.

I see them on the way, climbing the toilsome ascent. Jesus is calling on God in prayer, praying even for His murderers. And now they have gotten Him to the summit of the hill. They've arrived; it is Golgotha, the place of the skull. And they take and lay Him down on the cross. Yonder come the soldiers with hammers and nails in their hands. You can see them take those pliant arms and stretch them out, and against those blessed, innocent hands they point the sharp spikes. You can hear that hammer come down on that nail—blow, blow—and the hands of Jesus are pierced through, fastened bleeding to the cross. Long spikes are driven through both feet, and God, the Son of the Father, lies quivering, nailed to the cross. And now they mock at Him. See, they spit on Him, hooting and laughing and yelling, "Away with him; he saved others; let him save himself if he be Christ the chosen of God."

Then the Roman soldiers lifted up the cross and placed it upright between heaven and earth, with those arms of Jesus outstretched still in blessing. The love that

He had in His bosom kept those dear hands extended; they didn't need the nails. He might have come down from the cross; with one stroke of His hand He could have summoned all the angels of God against His murderers, or called down fire out of heaven to consume every one of them. But no; He willed to hang there between heaven and earth; His strength fainted not. Even "as Moses lifted up the serpent in the wilderness, even so must the Son of man be lifted up, that whosoever believeth in him should not perish but have everlasting life." O sinner, go to Calvary tonight; look on that Savior; gaze on Him between those two thieves; hear that piercing cry—does He call down fire from heaven? No, no! "Father, Father," He cries, "forgive them, for they know not what they do." Yes, I think that Christ did forgive from His heart every soul there on Calvary, even those that drove the spikes, even those that wagged their heads and reviled Him. Even the two thieves railed on Him. But at last one of them cried out, "Lord, remember me when thou comest into thy kingdom." Oh, sinner, did Christ rebuke him, or did He keep silent? No; a benediction fell from His lips, "Today shalt thou be with me in paradise." That malefactor had but to cry and he was snatched from the brink of hell.

Oh, lost one, but cry tonight to Jesus, and He will save you. Will you not let Him? Oh, hear His gracious words to the vile malefactor, "This day shalt thou be with me in paradise." At last He cried out, "I thirst," and they gave him gall mixed with vinegar, and mocked Him again, "Hail, King of the Jews, come down from thy cross." But He patiently endured. And again He opens His lips, we hear that cry from that cross. "Father, into thy hands I commend my spirit." And then the end approaches, and He cries out in a loud voice: "It is finished." It is finished. It is finished.

What a thrill of joy must have swept through the streets of heaven. "It is finished! It is finished!" the angels cry as they strike their golden harps, and the bells of heaven, if there are any there, ring out the peal of joy. "It is finished, the whole world can now be saved. The work of the God-man is finished today on Calvary; all that man has to do is to believe and they shall be saved!"

The Son of man had triumphed; He had died to make atonement, and through Him all flesh might die and yet live eternally. The work was complete; the world was saved! Ah, I can just imagine how the black powers of hell gathered around that dying scene, and the waves of hell and death dashed upon that cross. Sometimes, down on the beach of Lake Michigan, there you see the waves coming dashing on the breakwater. They come dashing along as though they would break everything to pieces, but the waves themselves are dashed to pieces and the breakwater stands invincible. So the dark waves of death and hell come dashing up against the bosom of the Son of God. They roared and surged, but all in vain; they fell back shattered into fine spray against the Rock, Christ—Christ the destroyer of death, Christ the victor over hell. When He shouts, "It is finished," I think I see the fiend creeping back to hell and hear him whispering, "It is finished; all mankind can now be saved." They have led on the children to kill the Son of God; but they are out-witted, for God "maketh even the wrath of man to praise him."

But my friends, we will not leave Him there on the cross. We are told that straightway when He yielded up the ghost, even nature owned its God. The sun refused to look longer upon the scene; darkness came over the earth for three hours; the rocks were rent, and the earth was shaken, and many that slept came forth from their graves. And when Jesus was now dead, we are told that Joseph of Arimathea, a rich man and a member of the Sanhedrin, went boldly to Pilate and begged [for] the Lord's body that he might bury it. He was a just man, he was an honorable counselor, and let me mention right here a most remarkable thing: Matthew, Mark, Luke, and John all join in telling of this pious act of Joseph's. It is not everything in this story of the last agony that all four of them bring out, but they all give this: Joseph of Arimathea, the secret disciple, was left to ask for the Lord's body. All His open disciples had forsaken Him and fled; all had forsaken Him—some had disowned Him, and Judas had betrayed Him; and it was left for Joseph of Arimathea to go to Pilate and himself alone perform the last offices for the dead Master. It was the death of Jesus that brought out Joseph of Arimathea, the secret disciple—O backward, secret Christians, shall it not touch you too? My friends, if Christ died for you on Calvary, shall you not live for Him? Shall you not speak for Him? Is not this the least you can do?

He [Joseph] went boldly into the presence of the governor and asked him for the body of Jesus. When Pilate heard He was dead he marveled. He gave orders to see that Jesus was dead. And now you can see those Roman soldiers going toward Calvary and Joseph with some of his servants behind him. See them standing at the cross and a soldier just goes up and puts a spear into the side of the Son of God, and that prophecy was brought out: "In that day there shall be a fountain opened in the house of David for sin and for uncleanness." The soldier put it in, and His blood covered the spear. Yes, Christ's blood covered sin. Yes, God, in mercy, covered sin. That act was the crowning act of indignity of earth and hell to drive that spear into the very heart of the God-man; and the crowning act of mercy and love and heaven that blood came out and covered the spear.

And now Joseph and Nicodemus take down that body. You can see them wash the blood from that head, you can see them draw those nails out carefully from His hands—from His feet, and they take that mangled and bruised body down and wash it.

(At this moment the roaring wind, which had been rising all the evening, seemed as though it would break through the roof, to which point nearly everybody's attention was attracted.)

My friends, it is only the wind. The devil doesn't want you to hear this story of Jesus' dying love for you; he doesn't want you to hear and be saved. But just give attention, and don't let him accomplish his object; let the wind go. If you don't pay attention my sermon goes for nothing.

You see them take the body down and wrap it in fine linen. You can see Joseph of Arimathea and Nicodemus, another secret disciple, anoint that body with ointment, and then a little funeral procession moving to the tomb of Joseph, hewn out of the rock, and there they lay that body away.

But, thank God, He did not rest very long. I have not time to speak about His resurrection now, but, God willing, I will speak about it before I leave. But let me ask you, are you going out of this tabernacle saying you don't want Christ—saying you would rather be without Him? Are you going out despising His love, His death, His offer of mercy? "Christ died for our sins." Will you have the benefit of His death, or send the message back to the God of heaven that you despise His love, His offer of mercy, that you despise this blessed Redeemer that came down to seek and save that which was lost?

ML